CONFUCIUS
—the Secular as Sacred

the text of this book is printed
on 100% recycled paper

CONFUCIUS
—the Secular as Sacred

Herbert Fingarette

HARPER TORCHBOOKS
Harper & Row, Publishers
New York, Evanston, San Francisco, London

Contents

Preface

When I began to read Confucius, I found him to be a prosaic and parochial moralizer; his collected sayings, the *Analects*, seemed to me an archaic irrelevance. Later, and with increasing force, I found him a thinker with profound insight and with an imaginative vision of man equal in its grandeur to any I know. Increasingly, I have become convinced that Confucius can be a teacher to us today—a major teacher, not one who merely gives us a slightly exotic perspective on the ideas already current. He tells us things not being said elsewhere; things needing to be said. He has a new lesson to teach.

Having the benefit of some acquaintance with recent developments in the philosophical study of man, I also saw that there are distinctive insights in the *Analects*, which are close in substance and spirit to some of the most characteristic of the very recent philosophical developments. In these respects, then, he was "ahead of our times" until recently, and this is an important reason for his having been pretty much neglected in the West for several centuries. Now, however, we can profit from the parallels in his thinking to certain new strands of Western thought, for here his way of putting the issues places them in a fresh perspective.

In coming to the conclusion that there are such important parallels in addition to what is more radically new, I have tried to take into account the natural tendency to read into a text the ideas by which one is already seized. With what success this has been done, the reader will judge. I will only say here that my primary aim—and joy, when successful—has been to discover what is distinctive in Confucius, to learn what he can teach me, not to seek that somewhat pendantic pleasure we can find in showing that an ancient and alien teacher anticipated some point which is already quite familiar to us.

Among Confucius's earlier translators, learned Catholic scholars and priests and devout missionary Protestants, were men of intellectual integrity whom one can only respect for their great achievement. But they tended to admire Confucius in somewhat the way the Church used to admire Socrates—as one who, though pagan, was near saintliness in his dedication to the highest truths and most perfect life, but who, alas, aspired to what only Christian Revelation can bring to fruition. Where the *Analects* could be read as approximating Christian ethics, or as adumbrating Christian theology, Confucius, too, was found admirable. More to the point for present purposes—such readings were often favored in the translating. In any case, the text was read by men instinctively and still unself-consciously bound by thinking in Christian terms, in European terms.

In more recent times, more anthropologically sophisticated and secularly oriented scholars have applied themselves to translating the *Analects*. The specifically Christian element has disappeared in recent translations. But often the European background assumptions remain. Even where European ideas do not infect the translation, it is Buddhist and Taoist thought —now so much more familiar to Western scholars—which colors the rendering. Then the error is a cumulative one. For the Buddhist ideas, however different from European ideas in so many respects, share with the latter certain fundamental biases: they favor the individualistic and subjectivistic view of man. It is individual mind, the inner life and reality of the individual, which is focal in understanding man as viewed throughout the main course of Buddhist and European thinking. I realize, of course, that this latter statement is an enormous generalization, subject to many kinds of exception being taken. I offer it, however, in this spirit; after the studies that issued in this book, I appreciated new, and to me, powerfully illuminating ways in which that generalization can be supported and understood.

In any case it came to appear to me that whatever the other differences of emphasis among individual translators, the subjective-psychologistic reading of the *Analects* is presumed throughout in every translation, and it is presumed in a quite unself-conscious, and hence all the more prejudicial way. It is a thesis of the present book that with respect to this fundamental bias, all the extant translations have misled: if I am right, they have introduced a way of seeing man which is not that of Confucius, and they have, as a result, failed to bring out, nor do their translations even allow for, certain distinctively non-European, non-Buddhist features of Confucius's view of man.

In finding this to be so, and now in trying to show here why it is so, one of my principal resources has been the original text, to try to see what it says, what it implies and what it does not say or need not imply. The original text can say with absolute obviousness only so much. Beyond this one must ask questions of it, and one may get answers; but the unasked questions are unlikely to be answered. One who is mainly concerned with stylistic issues will provide a translation geared to rendering the stylistic nuances of the original but blurring, perhaps, the psychological ones. One who is primarily concerned with psychological issues may be less interested to bring out, and even less able to appreciate those stylistic nuances. No modern translation of the *Analects* has been done by a Westerner who is a professional philosopher.

In consequence, I believe, no translation has been inspired by an adequate familiarity with contemporary philosophical ideas and techniques.

It is with these remarks as background that I say I have tried to discover Confucius's teaching by taking him at his word. One further thing I mean by this is that I have tried to stay as strictly as possible within the confines of the earlier and purportedly more authentic passages of the *Analects,* mainly the first fifteen books out of the total of twenty; and even here I have been cautious about what scholars have taken to be later interpolations into these earliest passages. However, for my present purposes, it is not essential to insist that the historical Confucius said all or any of these "sayings." After eliminating certain passages in this spirit, on the basis of independent scholarly studies (see the appended Note on Textual Matters), we are left with a text that has unity in terms of historical-social context, linguistic style and philosophical content. It is this text, and this one only, that I have tried to interpret here.

I have refrained to the utmost from introducing interpretative material from what we know to be later Chinese commentaries; it seems to me that the cross-fertilization and fusion of quite different lines of philosophic thought in China in the age of the "Philosophers" quickly gave a different cast to what Confucius was saying. Of course such an attempt to reach Confucius pure can only succeed in degree, never completely. *All* our texts and readings are irremediably infected with interpretation, commentary, editorial selection and sheer ideological skullduggery.

Ultimately, however, my interest is philosophical, and therefore what counts for me is the philosophical insight in the chosen text when it is responsibly read. And I have always tried to keep this in mind even though, as my remarks have already suggested, I believe one cannot completely divorce a responsible philosophical reading of such a text from careful historical and linguistic analysis. Furthermore, it is consistent with my purposes and method that, not being a Sinologist myself, I have relied heavily on secondary materials and commentary by Western scholars, including, of course, their often excellent summaries of the vast lore of Chinese scholarship. But in my principal chosen task—the intensive and careful philosophical study of the *Analects*—I have done my own reading in the original text. Wherever relevant philosophical problems were rooted in textual problems, there I have done my own independent textual analysis so far as I believed it relevant to the philosophical point of that text.

I must therefore bear responsibility for the translations of passages offered here, though they are based upon wide consultation, heavy borrowing, and in a number of cases, simple quotation from leading translations and scholarly articles. My main object has been to select translations or to retranslate with an eye toward bringing out the philosophical nuances of the text. In some instances, these are in the nature of specific notions or implications distinctly present (though not always immediately evident). In other cases, and equally important, what is philosophically relevant is the ambiguity, vagueness, silence or other evidence of unconcern in the text with respect to distinctions that thinkers in other traditions might regularly introduce and attempt to be clear about. Naturally I have discussed the text and the issues in order to bring out my reasons for a philosophically critical point of translation, and I believe I have avoided what would be considered eccentric renderings designed to force the meaning in order to support my thesis.

I

Human Community as Holy Rite

The remarks which follow are aimed at revealing the magic power which Confucius saw, quite correctly, as the very essence of human virtue. It is finally by way of the magical that we can also arrive at the best vantage point for seeing the holiness in human existence which Confucius saw as central. In the twentieth century this central role of the holy in Confucius's teaching has been largely ignored because we have failed to grasp the existential point of that teaching.

Specifically, what is needed (and is here proposed) is a reinterpretation which makes use of contemporary philosophical understanding. In fact such a reinterpretation casts, by reflection as it were, illumination into dimensions of our own philosophical thought, which have remained in shadow.

The distinctive philosophical insight in the *Analects*, or at least in its more authentic "core," was quickly obscured as the ideas of rival schools infected Confucius's teaching. It is not surprising that this insight, requiring as it does a certain emphasis on the magical and religious dimensions of the *Analects*, is absent from the usual Western-influenced interpretations of modern times. Today the *Analects* is read, in its main drift, either as an empirical, humanist, this-worldly teaching or as a parallel to Platonist-rationalist doctrines. Indeed, the teaching of the *Analects* is often viewed as a major step toward the explicit rejection of superstition or heavy reliance on "supernatural forces."[1]

There is no doubt that the world of the *Analects* is profoundly different in its quality from that of Moses, Aeschylus, Jesus, Gautama Buddha, Lao-tzu or the Upanishadic teachers. In certain obvious respects the *Analects* does indeed represent the world of a humanist and a traditionalist, one who is, however, sufficiently traditional to render a kind of pragmatic homage, when necessary, to the spirits.

"Devote yourself to man's duties," says the Master; "respect spiritual beings but keep distance." (6:20)* He suited the deed to the precept and himself "never talked of prodigies, feats of strength, disorders, or spirits." (7:20) In response to direct questions about the transcendental and supernatural he said: "Until you are able to serve men, how can you serve spiritual being? Until you know about life, how can you know about death?" (11:11)

If we examine the substance of the *Analects* text, it is quickly evident that the topics and the chief concepts pertain primarily to our human nature, comportment and relationships. Merely to list some of the constantly recurring themes suffices for our present purposes: Rite *(li)*, Humaneness *(jen)*, Reciprocity *(shu)*, Loyalty *(chung)*, Learning *(hsueh)*, Music *(yüeh)*, and the concepts by which are defined the familial-

---

1. In this middle third of the twentieth century, writers who disagree in many ways almost all tend to agree on the secular, humanist, rationalist orientation of Confucius. Waley says the turn toward the this-worldly was characteristic of tendencies of the age and not peculiar to Confucius. See Waley, *Analects of Confucius*, pp. 32–33. See also Leslie, *Confucius*, pp. 40–41; Chan, *Source Book*, p. 15; H. G. Creel, *Confucius and the Chinese Way*, p. 120; Kaizuka, pp. 109–119; Liu, *Confucius, His Life and Times*, pp. 154–156. Yu-lan Fung, in his various pre-Communist works, takes a more ambiguous position on this issue but seems to me to stress the rationalist, humanist aspects, ending by holding this to be a defect of one-sidedness in Confucius; cf. his *The Spirit of Chinese Philosophy*, p. 28.

*Quotations from the *Analects* are cited by chapter and paragraph according to the traditional text.

social relationships and obligations (prince, father, etc.).

The this-worldly, practical humanism of the *Analects* is further deepened by the teaching that the moral and spiritual achievements of man do not depend on tricks or luck or on esoteric spells or on any purely external agency. One's spiritual condition depends on the "stuff" one has to begin with, on the amount and quality of study and good hard work one puts into "shaping" it. Spiritual nobility calls for persistence and effort. "First the difficult. . . ." (6:20) "His burden is heavy and his course is long. He has taken *jen* as his burden —is that not heavy?"(8:7) What disquieted Confucius was "leaving virtue untended and learning unperfected, hearing about what is right but not managing either to turn toward it or to reform what is evil."(7:3) The disciple of Confucius was surely all too aware that his task was one calling not for amazement and miracle but for constant "cutting, filing, carving, polishing" (1:15) in order to become a fully and truly human being, a worthy participant in society. All this seems the very essence of the antimagical in outlook. Nor does it have the aura of the Divine.

Yet, in spite of this dedicated and apparently secular prosaic moralism, we also find occasional comments in the *Analects* which seem to reveal a belief in magical powers of profound importance. By "magic" I mean the power of a specific person to accomplish his will directly and effortlessly through ritual, gesture and incantation. The user of magic does not work by strategies and devices as a means toward an end; he does not use coercion or physical forces. There are no pragmatically developed and tested strategies or tactics. He simply wills the end in the proper ritual setting and with the proper ritual gesture and word; without further effort on his part, the deed is accomplished. Confucius's words at times strongly suggest some fundamental magical power as central to this way. (In the following citations, the Chinese terms all are central to

Confucius's thought, and they designate powers, states and forms of action of fundamental value. Insofar as necessary, they will be discussed later.)

"Is *jen* far away? As soon as I want it, it is here." (7:29)

"Self-disciplined and ever turning to *li*—everyone in the world will respond to his *jen.*" (12:1)

Shun, the great sage-ruler, "merely placed himself gravely and reverently with his face due South (the ruler's ritual posture); that was all" (i.e., and the affairs of his reign proceeded without flaw). (15:4)

The magical element always involves great effects produced effortlessly, marvelously, with an irresistible power that is itself intangible, invisible, unmanifest. "With correct comportment, no commands are necessary, yet affairs proceed."(13:6) "The character of a noble man is like wind, that of ordinary men like grass; when the wind blows the grass must bend."(12:19) "To govern by *te* is to be like the North Polar Star; it remains in place while all the other stars revolve in homage about it."(2:1)

Such comments can be taken in various ways. One may simply note that, as Duyvendak remarks, the "original magical meaning" of 2:1 is "unmistakable," or that the ritual posture of Shun in 15:4 is "a state of the highest magical potency."[2] In short, one may admit that these are genuine residues of "superstition" in the *Analects*.

However, many modern interpreters of the *Analects* have wished to read Confucius more "sympathetically," that is, as one whose philosophic claims would have maximum validity for us in our own familiar and accepted terms. To do this these commentators have generally tried to minimize to the irreducible the magical claims in the *Analects*. For it is accepted as

2. J. L. Duyvendak, "The Philosophy of Wu Wei," *Études Asiatiques* 3/4 (1947), p. 84.

an axiom in our times that the goal of direct action by incantation and ritual gesture cannot be taken as a serious possibility.
(The important exception to this general acceptance of the
axiom, to be discussed later, is contemporary "linguistic analysis." But the import of this work has as yet hardly extended
beyond the world of professional philosophy.)

The suggestion of magic and marvel so uncongenial to the
contemporary taste may be dissipated in various ways: only
one of the sayings I have quoted comes from the portion of the
Analects—Books 3 to 8—that has been most widely of all accepted as "authentic" in the main. The other sayings might be
among the many interpolations, often alien in spirit to Confucius, which are known to be in the received text. Or one might
hold that the magical element is quite restricted in scope,
applying only to the ruler or even the perfect ruler alone.[3] Still
another possible method of "interpreting away" the "magical"
statements is to suppose that Confucius was merely emphasizing and dramatizing the otherwise familiar power of setting a
good example.[4] In short, on this view we must take the "magical" sayings as being poetic statements of a prosaic truth.
Finally, one might simply argue that Confucius was not consistent on the issue—perhaps that he was mainly and characteristically antimagic, but, as might well be expected, he had
not entirely freed himself of deep-rooted traditional beliefs.

All of these interpretations take the teaching of a magical
dimension to human virtue as an obstacle to acceptance by the
sophisticated citizen of the twentieth century. The magic
must be interpreted away or else treated as a historically un-
derstandable failure on Confucius's part. I prefer to think we
can still learn from Confucius on this issue if we do not begin

3. Cf. Waley, *Analects of Confucius*, pp. 64–66, and especially "I do not think
Confucius attributed this magic power to any rites save those practiced by the
divinely appointed ruler."
4. See, for example, Ibid., p. 66.

by supposing the obvious meaning of his words as unacceptable.

Rather than engage in polemics regarding these other interpretations, I shall devote the remainder of my remarks to a positive exposition of what I take to be the genuine and sound magical view of man in Confucius's teaching. I do not hold that my interpretation is correct to the exclusion of all others. There is no reason to suppose that an innovator such as Confucius distinguishes all possible meanings of what he says and consciously intends only one of these meanings to the exclusion of all others. One should assume the contrary. Of the various meanings of the Confucian magical teaching, I believe the one to be elaborated in the following remarks is authentic, central and still unappreciated.

Confucius saw, and tried to call to our attention, that the truly, distinctively human powers have, characteristically, a magical quality. His task, therefore, required, in effect, that he reveal what is already so familiar and universal as to be unnoticed. What is necessary in such cases is that one come upon this "obvious" dimension of our existence in a new way, in the right way. Where can one find such a new path to this familiar area, one which provides a new and revealing perspective? Confucius found the path: we go by way of the notion of *li*.

One has to labor long and hard to learn *li*. The word in its root meaning is close to "holy ritual," "sacred ceremony." Characteristic of Confucius's teaching is the use of the language and imagery of *li* as a medium within which to talk about the entire body of the *mores*, or more precisely, of the authentic tradition and reasonable conventions of society.[5] Confucius taught that the ability to act according to *li* and the will to submit to *li* are essential to that perfect and peculiarly

---

5. See, for example, H. G. Creel, *Confucius*, pp. 82–83. See also, *Analects*, 9:3.

human virtue or power which can be man's. Confucius thus does two things here: he calls our attention to the entire body of tradition and convention, and he calls upon us to see all this by means of a metaphor, through the imagery of sacred ceremony, holy rite.

The (spiritually) noble man is one who has labored at the alchemy of fusing social forms *(li)* and raw personal existence in such a way that they transmuted into a way of being which realizes *te*, the distinctively human virtue or power.

Te is realized in concrete acts of human intercourse, the acts being of a pattern. These patterns have certain general features, features common to all such patterns of *li:* they are all expressive of "man-to-man-ness," of reciprocal loyalty and respect. But the patterns are also specific: they differentiate and they define in detail the ritual performance-repertoires which constitute civilized, i.e., truly human patterns of mourning, marrying and fighting, of being a prince, a father, a son and so on. However, men are by no means conceived as being mere standardized units mechanically carrying out prescribed routines in the service of some cosmic or social law. Nor are they self-sufficient, individual souls who happen to consent to a social contract. Men become truly human as their raw impulse is shaped by *li.* And *li* is the fulfillment of human impulse, the civilized expression of it—not a formalistic dehumanization. *Li* is the specifically humanizing form of the dynamic relation of man-to-man.

The novel and creative insight of Confucius was to see this aspect of human existence, its form as learned tradition and convention, in terms of a particular revelatory image: *li,* i.e, "holy rite," "sacred ceremony," in the usual meaning of the term prior to Confucius.

In well-learned ceremony, each person does what he is supposed to do according to a pattern. My gestures are coordinated harmoniously with yours—though neither of us has to force, push, demand, compel or otherwise "make" this happen. Our gestures are in turn smoothly followed by those of the other participants, all effortlessly. If all are "self-disciplined, ever turning to *li*," then all that is needed—quite literally—is an initial ritual gesture in the proper ceremonial context; from there onward everything "happens." What action did Shun (the Sage-ruler) take? "He merely placed himself gravely and reverently with his face due south; that was all." (15:4) Let us consider in at least a little detail the distinctive features of action emphasized by this revelatory image of Holy Rite.

It is important that we do not think of this effortlessness as "mechanical" or "automatic." If it is so, then, as Confucius repeatedly indicates, the ceremony is dead, sterile, empty: there is no *spirit* in it. The truly ceremonial "takes place"; there is a kind of spontaneity. It happens "of itself." There is life in it because the individuals involved do it with seriousness and sincerity. For ceremony to be authentic one must "participate in the sacrifice"; otherwise it is as if one "did not sacrifice at all."(3:12) To put it another way, there are two contrasting kinds of failure in carrying out *li:* the ceremony may be awkwardly performed for lack of learning and skill; or the ceremony may have a surface slickness but yet be dull, mechanical for lack of serious purpose and commitment. Beautiful and effective ceremony requires the personal "presence" to be fused with learned ceremonial skill. This ideal fusion is true *li* as sacred rite.

Confucius characteristically and sharply contrasts the ruler who uses *li* with the ruler who seeks to attain his ends by means of commands, threats, regulations, punishments and force. (2:3) The force of coercion is manifest and tangible, whereas the vast (and sacred) forces at work in *li* are invisible and intangible. *Li* works through spontaneous coordination rooted in reverent dignity. The perfection in

Holy Rite is esthetic as well as spiritual.

Having considered holy ceremony in itself, we are now prepared to turn to more everyday aspects of life. This is in effect what Confucius invites us to do; it is the foundation for his perspective on man.

I see you on the street; I smile, walk toward you, put out my hand to shake yours. And behold—without any command, stratagem, force, special tricks or tools, without any effort on my part to make you do so, you spontaneously turn toward me, return my smile, raise your hand toward mine. We shake hands—not by my pulling your hand up and down or your pulling mine but by spontaneous and perfect cooperative action. Normally we do not notice the subtlety and amazing complexity of this coordinated "ritual" act. This subtlety and complexity become very evident, however, if one has had to learn the ceremony only from a book of instructions, or if one is a foreigner from a nonhandshaking culture.

Nor normally do we notice that the "ritual" has "life" in it, that we are "present" to each other, at least to some minimal extent. As Confucius said, there are always the general and fundamental requirements of reciprocal good faith and respect. This mutual respect is not the same as a conscious feeling of mutual respect; when I am *aware* of a respect for you, I am much more likely to be piously fatuous or perhaps self-consciously embarrassed; and no doubt our little "ceremony" will reveal this in certain awkwardnesses. (I put out my hand too soon and am left with it hanging in midair.) No, the authenticity of the mutual respect does not require that I consciously feel respect or focus my attention on my respect for you; it is fully expressed in the correct "live" and spontaneous performance of the *act*. Just as an aerial acrobat must, at least for the purpose at hand, possess (but not think about his) complete trust in his partner if the trick is to come off, so we who shake hands, though the stakes are less, must have (but not think about) respect and trust. Otherwise we find ourselves fumbling awkwardly or performing in a lifeless fashion, which easily conveys its meaninglessness to the other.

Clearly it is not necessary that our reciprocal respect and good faith go very far in order for us to accomplish a reasonably successful handshake and greeting. Yet even here, the sensitive person can often plumb the depths of another's attitude from a handshake. This depth of human relationship expressible in a "ceremonial" gesture is in good part possible because of the remarkable specificity of the ceremony. For example, if I am your former teacher, you will spontaneously be rather obvious in walking toward me rather than waiting for me to walk toward you. You will allow a certain subtle reserve in your handshake, even though it will be warm. You will not slap me on the back, though conceivably I might grasp you by the shoulder with my free hand. There are indescribably many subtleties in the distinctions, nuances and minute but meaningful variations in gesture. If we do try to describe these subtle variations and their rules, we immediately sound like Book 10 of the *Analects*, whose ceremonial recipes initially seem to the modern American reader to be the quintessence of quaint and extreme traditionalism. It is in just such ways that social activity is coordinated in civilized society, without effort or planning, but simply by spontaneously initiating the appropriate ritual gesture in an appropriate setting. This power of *li*, Confucius says, depends upon prior learning. It is not inborn.

The effortless power of *li* can also be used to accomplish physical ends, though we usually do not think of it this way. Let us suppose I wish to bring a book from my office to my classroom. If I have no magic powers, I must literally take steps—walk to my office, push the door open, lift the book with my own muscles, physically carry it back. But there is also magic—the proper ritual expression of my wish which will accomplish my wish with no such effort on my part. I turn politely, i.e., ceremonially, to one of my students in class and merely express in an appropriate and polite (ritual) formula my wish that he bring me the book. This proper ceremonial expression of my wish is all; I do not need to force him, threaten him, trick him. I do not need to do anything more myself. In almost no time the book is in my hands, as I wished! This is a uniquely human way of getting things done.

The examples of handshaking and of making a request are humble; the moral is profound. These complex but familiar gestures are characteristic of human relationships at their most human: we are least like anything else in the world when we do not treat each other as physical objects, as animals or even as subhuman creatures to be driven, threatened, forced, maneuvered. Looking at these "ceremonies" through the image of *li*, we realize that explicitly sacred rite can be seen as an emphatic, intensified and sharply elaborated extension of everyday *civilized* intercourse.

The notion that we can use speech only to talk *about* action or indirectly to *evoke* action has dominated modern Western thought. Yet contemporary "linguistic" analysis in philosophy has revealed increasingly how much the ritual word is itself the critical act rather than a report of, or stimulus to, action. The late Professor J. L. Austin was one of those who brought the reality and pervasiveness of this phenomenon to a focus in his analyses of what he called the "performative utterance."[6] These are the innumerable statements we make

6. J. L. Austin, "Performative Utterances," in *Philosophical Papers* (London: Oxford University Press, 1961), pp. 220–239; *How to Do Things with Words* (London: Oxford University Press, 1962); "Performatif-Constatif," in *La Philosophie Analytique*, Cahiers de Royaumont, Phil. No. V (Editions de Mincit, Paris, 1962), 271–305.

I have offered a systematic analysis of the concept of the performative, which I believe concords with and amplifies the points I am here making in connection with Confucius, though my analysis of performativeness was in-which function somewhat like the "operative" clause in a legal instrument. They are statements, but they are not statements *about* some act or inviting some action; instead they are the very execution of the act itself.

"I give and bequeath my watch to my brother," duly said or written is not a report of what I have already done but is the very act of bequeathal itself. In a marriage ceremony, the "I do" is not a report of an inner mental act of acceptance; it is itself the act which seals my part of the bargain. "I promise . . ." is not a report of what I have done a moment before inside my head, nor is it indeed a report of anything at all; the uttering of the words is itself the act of promising. It is by words, and by the ceremony of which the words form a part, that I bind myself in a way which, for a man "ever turning to *li*," is more powerful, more inescapable than strategies or force. Confucius truly tells us that the man who uses the power of *li* can influence those above him—but not the man who has only physical force at his command.

There is no power of *li* if there is no learned and accepted convention, or if we utter the words and invoke the power of the convention in an inappropriate setting, or if the ceremony is not fully carried out, or if the persons carrying out the ceremonial roles are not those properly authorized ("authorization"—again a ceremony). In short, the peculiarly moral yet binding power of ceremonial gesture and word cannot be abstracted from or used in isolation from ceremony. It is not a distinct power we happen to use in ceremony; it is the power *of* ceremony. I cannot effectively go through the ceremony of bequeathing my servant to someone if, in our society, there is no accepted convention of slavery; I cannot bet two dollars if no one completes the bet by accepting; I cannot legally plead

---

tended to be entirely general. See Herbert Fingarette, "Performatives," *American Philosophical Quarterly*, Vol. 4 (1967).

"Guilty" to a crime while eating dinner at home. Thus the power of *li* cannot be used except as the *li* is fully respected. This, too, is Confucius's constant refrain. "The Three Families used the Yung Song . . . what possible application can such words have in the Hall of the Three Families?" (who were not entitled, according to *li*, to use this Song). (3:2)

For present purposes it is enough to note how many are the obvious performative formulas in our own language and ceremony,[7] and also to note that there may be less obvious but no less important performative formulas, for example, those formulas in which one expresses one's own wish or preference or choice. "I choose this one" excludes the objection, made after one receives it, that one was not speaking truly. For to say it in the proper circumstances is not to report something already done but is to take the "operative" step in making the choice.[8]

The upshot of this approach to language and its "ceremonial" context was, in the reasoning of Professor Austin, paradoxical. He came to feel forced toward the conclusion that ultimately *all* utterances are in some essential way performative. This remains an open question, but it suffices for us to recall that it is now a commonplace of contemporary analytical philosophy (as it was a basic thesis of pragmatist philosophies) that we use words to *do* things, profoundly important and amazingly varied things.

Indeed, the central lesson of these new philosophical insights is not so much a lesson about language as it is about

7. Though the list could go on interminably, I mention here just a few more terms which commonly enter into formulas having an obvious performative function: "I christen you," "I appoint you," "I pick this (or him)," "I congratulate you," "I welcome you," "I authorize you," "I challenge you," "I order you," "I request you."
8. For an extensive and characteristic example of the recent trend to treat as a special, crucial category these and other first-person present-tense expressions using "mental" or "action" verbs, see S. Hampshire, *Thought and Action* (London: Chatto & Windus, 1959).

ceremony. What we have come to see, in our own way, is how vast is the area of human existence in which the substance of that existence *is* the ceremony. Promises, commitments, excuses, pleas, compliments, pacts—these and so much more are ceremonies or they are nothing. It is thus in the medium of ceremony that the peculiarly human part of our life is lived. The ceremonial act is the primary, irreducible event;[9] language cannot be understood in isolation from the conventional practice in which it is rooted; conventional practice cannot be understood in isolation from the language that defines and is part of it. No purely physical motion is a promise; no word alone, independent of ceremonial context, circumstances and roles can be a promise. Word and motion are only abstractions from the concrete ceremonial act.

From this standpoint, it is easy to see that not only motor skills must be learned but also correct use of language. For correct use of language is *constitutive* of effective action as gesture is. Correct language is not merely a useful adjunct; it

9. The literature on issues pertaining to this topic is now vast, and in general one might summarize by saying that there are two distinct and contrasting trends, easily the two most influential throughout the English-speaking philosophical world. One trend is the "formalistic" analysis of science, language, and "knowledge," a kind of analysis which, in a much more attenuated and sophisticated way, still leans toward a view, opposed to what I have here expressed, that denies the ultimate irreducibility of such notions as, e.g., "the ceremonial act" and argues instead for a behavioral or physicalist approach to human conduct. I have in mind here the movement inspired by Russell and Whitehead's *Principia Mathematica* and by the work of the "Vienna Circle"; the more specific and recent tendencies may be sampled in such standard anthologies as that of H. Feigl and M. Brodbeck, *Readings in the Philosophy of Science* (New York: Appleton-Century-Crofts, 1953); and in the series of the Minnesota Studies in Philosophy of Science. The other trend has its roots in the later work of L. Wittgenstein, G. Ryle, J. L. Austin, P. F. Strawson, John Wisdom and others. These analysts have concentrated on the natural languages (hence not "formal" languages) and have in one way or another argued that the physicalist-behavioralist approaches to "mind" and "action" are fundamentally misconceived. They have been elaborating in great detail alternative analyses which, though not identical, have family resemblances and which affirm a radical, logical gap between the language of "action," "mind" and, in effect, what I have here called the ceremonial act and on the other hand the mathematical-physical language of physical science.

is of the essence of executing the ceremony.

From this perspective we see that the famous Confucian doctrine of *cheng ming*, the "rectification of terms" or "correct use of terminology," is not merely an erroneous belief in word-magic or a pedantic elaboration of Confucius's concern with teaching tradition. Nor do I see any reason to read into it a doctrine of "essences" or Platonic Ideas, or analogous medieval-age neo-Confucian notions, for the *Analects* provides no other hint of any such doctrine.[10]

Of course we must be leery of reading our own contemporary philosophical doctrines into an ancient teaching. Yet I think that the text of the *Analects*, in letter and spirit, supports and enriches our own quite recently emerging vision of man as a ceremonial being.

In general, what Confucius brings out in connection with the workings of ceremony is not only its distinctively human character, its linguistic and magical character, but also its

10. This position is taken more or less explicitly in the various works of Fung Yu-lan. The *Analects* passage which is most explicit—indeed the only fully explicit passage on *cheng ming* in the *Analects* (13:3)—is evidently much later in style than and different in content from the core of the work. See Waley, *Analects of Confucius*, p. 172. Even so, the passage does not itself say that names must "correspond" to "actualities" (Fung, *Chinese Philosophy*, p. 60); also essentially Chu Hsi's interpretation in his commentary on the Lun Yu. Nor does it say names must be in "accordance with the truth" (Legge), nor that "language must concord with what is meant" (Waley). The text itself merely says that names (or language) must be concordant (what is needed, or what goes with). But this leaves it ambiguous: Must language be concordant with the activity *(li)* of which it is a part ("the prince *being* a prince"), or must it concord as name with thing named? My own view is that the distinction was not originally clear, and that both senses were tacitly in mind. Even in Hsun Tzu, if one reads carefully with this question in mind, the issue is not clearly formulated one way or another, though he is always read as if he were definitely speaking of name and thing named. But this is in large part due to our own Western bias toward this traditional (but now widely rejected) doctrine of how language works; it is supported by the analogous view which also developed in China and becomes part of the orthodox commentary. Once we are aware of the ceremonial or performative kinds of functions of language, the original texts begin to read differently.

moral and religious character. Here, finally, we must recall and place at the focus of our analysis the fact that for Confucius it is the imagery of Holy Ceremony that unifies and infuses all these dimensions of human existence. Perhaps a modern Westerner would be tempted to speak of the "intelligent practice of learned conventions and language." This has a fashionably value-free, "scientific" ring. Indeed the contemporary analytical philosophers tend to speak this way and to be suitably common-sensical and restrained in their style. But this quite fails to accomplish what Confucius's central image did.

The image of Holy Rite as a metaphor of human existence brings foremost to our attention the dimension of the holy in man's existence. There are several dimensions of Holy Rite which culminate in its holiness. Rite brings out forcefully not only the harmony and beauty of social forms, the inherent and ultimate dignity of human intercourse; it brings out also the moral perfection implicit in achieving one's ends by dealing with others as beings of equal dignity, as free coparticipants in *li*. Furthermore, to act by ceremony is to be completely open to the other; for ceremony is public, shared, transparent; to act otherwise is to be secret, obscure and devious, or merely tyrannically coercive. It is in this beautiful and dignified, shared and open participation with others who are ultimately like oneself (12:2) that man realizes himself. Thus perfect community of men—the Confucian analogue to Christian brotherhood—becomes an inextricable part, the chief aspect, of Divine worship—again an analogy with the central Law taught by Jesus.

Confucius wanted to teach us, as a corollary, that sacred ceremony in its narrower, root meaning is not a totally mysterious appeasement of spirits external to human and earthly life. Spirit is no longer an external being influenced by the ceremony; it is that that is expressed and comes most alive *in* the ceremony. Instead of being diversion of attention from the human realm to another transcendent realm, the overtly holy ceremony is to be seen as the central symbol, both expressive of and participating in the holy as a dimension of all truly human existence. Explicitly Holy Rite is thus a luminous point of concentration in the greater and ideally all-inclusive ceremonial harmony of the perfectly humane civilization of the *Tao*, or ideal Way. Human life in its entirety finally appears as one vast, spontaneous and holy Rite: the community of man. This, for Confucius, was indeed an "ultimate concern"; it was, he said, again and again, the only thing that mattered, more than the individual's life itself. (3:17; 4:5, 6, 8)

2

A Way
without a Crossroads

Confucius in his teachings in the *Analects* does not elaborate on the language of choice or responsibility. He occasionally uses terms roughly akin to these. But they are not developed or elaborated in the ways so characteristic of their central import in Western philosophical and religious understanding of man. To be specific, Confucius does not elaborate the language of choice and responsibility as these are intimately intertwined with the idea of the ontologically ultimate power of the individual to select from genuine alternatives to create his own spiritual destiny, and with the related ideas of spiritual guilt, and repentance or retribution for such guilt.

Precisely because we of the West are so deeply immersed in a world conceived in just such terms, it is profitable for us to see the world in quite another way, in Confucius's way. He was, after all, profoundly concerned to understand man and man's place in society. He was dedicated to defining and illuminating what we would call moral issues. He was a great and an original teacher. How, then, could Confucius omit this whole complex of notions centering around "choice" and "responsibility"?

We must recognize at once that the absence of a developed language of choice and responsibility does not imply a failure to choose or to be responsible. Some men were more responsible than others in Confucius's day as in ours. It is also obvious that men made choices in ancient China. I am not so sure we can speak as confidently about guilt, repentance or retributive punishment in the sense we use these words, but also the realities which we use these words to designate did not exist. The notion of punishment, which did exist in ancient China, was that of deterrent punishment—not due retribution to cleanse guilt, but a stern "lesson" or literal crippling which would deter future malfeasance.

However, without arguing this latter point here, we can allow that in the case of "choice" and "responsibility," the realities they designate did indeed exist. Yet, although we in the West have an elaborated language in which to express these realities and to trace out their inner shape and dynamics in detail, Confucius (and his contemporaries) did not possess such a language. And they had no significant concern with these moral realities so central to their contemporaries, the peoples of Greece and the Near East.

Perhaps the most revealing way to begin to bring out this "omission" is to consider the primary imagery in the *Analects*. It centers around the *"Tao."* Tao is a Way, a path, a road, and by common metaphorical extensions it becomes in ancient China the right Way of life, the Way of governing, the ideal Way of human existence, the Way of the Cosmos, the generative-normative Way (Pattern, path, course) of existence as such. (In the *Analects*, *"Tao"* never takes its rare but possible alternative sense as "word" or "speak.")

The imagery in the *Analects* is dominated by the metaphor of traveling the road. Written characters that occur typically and frequently in the text are those meaning path, way, walk, tracks, follow, go through, from, to, enter, leave, arrive, advance, upright, crooked, level, smooth, stop, position.

The notion of a Way is, not surprisingly, congenial to the central Confucian notion of *li*, rite or ceremony. *Li*, for Confucius, is the explicit and detailed pattern of that great ceremony which is social intercourse, the humane life. The transition from the image of walking the true Path uprightly to carrying out a ceremony properly is an easy and congenial one. We may even think of *li* as the map or the specific road-system which is *Tao*.

It is easy, if one is so inclined, to develop this path-imagery to bring in the notions of choice, decision, responsibility. We should need only to introduce the derivative image of the crossroads, an obvious elaboration of *Tao* imagery to us. Yet this image, so perfectly suited, so plainly available for use as a metaphor for choice, is *never* used in the *Analects*.

Indeed the image of the crossroads is so natural and even insistently available as an element of any richly elaborated path-imagery that only the most profound commitment to the idea of the cosmos as basically unambiguous, as a single, definite order, could make it possible to ignore in the metaphor the image of the crossroads as a challenge to the traveler on the Way. This Confucian commitment to a single, definite order is also evident when we note what Confucius sees as the alternative to rightly treading the true Path: it is to walk crookedly, to get lost or to abandon the Path. That is, the only "alternative" to the one Order is disorder, chaos.

Where does one finally arrive if one follows the Way? Is there a goal that puts an end to the travel? The imagery of Confucius does not lead us to dwell upon the person arriving at a destined or ideal place, whether it be depicted as harbor, home or golden city. Instead, the spiritually noble man arrives at a condition rather than a place, the condition of following the Way without effort and properly. He arrives at that tranquil state that comes from appreciating that it is the following of the Way itself that is of ultimate and absolute value. Thus in this respect it does not take time to "reach" the goal since one does not have to arrive at any particular point on the map:

to reach the goal is simply to set oneself to treading the Path now—properly, with correct appreciation of its intrinsic and ultimate significance.

One can be truly following the Way at whatever the level of one's personal development and skill in the Way, whatever the level of one's learning—for a wholehearted commitment to learning the Way is itself the Way for those who are not yet perfected in the Way. However, although the learner may be following the Way for the learner, he cannot rest; his burden is heavy for he is the apprentice, not yet the Master, the *jen* man, the man perfected in *li*, the truly noble man.

The basic conception of man in the *Analects* is that he is a being born into the world—more especially into society—with the potentiality to be shaped into a truly human form. There is, to begin with, the raw stuff, the raw material. This must be elaborated by learning and culture, shaped and controlled by *li*. Either this "cutting, filing, chiseling and polishing" (1:15) is done well or poorly. If it is well done, through painstaking and properly directed effort by the person and good training by his teachers, then to that extent he will walk straight upon the Way. If there is a failure to shape according to the ideal, then by virtue of this defect he will deviate from the Way.

Thus there is no *genuine* option: either one follows the Way or one fails. To take any other "route" than the Way is not a genuine road but a failure through weakness to follow *the* route. Neither the doctrine nor the imagery allows for choice, if we mean by choice a selection, by virtue of the agent's powers, of one out of several equally real options. Instead it puts the task in terms of either using one's powers to walk the Way or being too weak, *without* power, and of going crookedly nowhere, falling or weaving about pointlessly in quest of the mirages of profit, advantage and personal comfort.

It is true that the Master said: "If a man doesn't constantly

ask himself, 'What about this, what about this?' I can do nothing about him." (15:15) Our own tendency, reading this isolated
remark, may be to read this as a concern with choice. But it
need not be so at all. It need not be read as "What about this
—which of the alternatives, to do it or not to do it, shall I
choose?" Instead, one may suppose that the notion of equally
valid alternatives is not implied, that there is presumed to be
only one right thing to do and that the question then means
in effect, "What about this, *is* it right; is it the Way?" Put in
more general terms, the task is not conceived as a choice but
as the attempt to characterize some object or action as objectively right or not. The moral task is to make a proper classifi-
cation, to locate an act within the scheme of *li*.

There are two passages in the *Analects* in which Confucius comments on a matter that can be rendered as a mind
"deluded" or in "error" or in "doubt," but which Waley
translates as a matter of "deciding when in two minds." Although Waley's translation makes choice or decision the issue, the Master's elaboration of the notion reveals, I believe, that Waley's rendering is misleading for purposes of
a philosophical understanding of Confucius. In both passages (12:10, 12:21), the meaning is not that of a mind in
doubt as to which course to choose but of a person being
inconsistent in his desires or acts. Paraphrasing the theme
of these texts: one wants someone—perhaps a relative—to
live and prosper, but out of anger, one wishes that he per-
ish or one actually endangers him out of a blind rage. In
such conflict, the task is not posed as one of *choosing* or *deciding* but of distinguishing or *discriminating (pien)* the inconsistent inclinations. Furthermore, in each passage, we
have no doubt about which inclination is the right one
when we have discriminated one from the other. In short,
the task is posed in terms of knowledge rather than choice.
Huo, the key term in the passages, means here "deluded or

led astray by an un-*li* inclination or tendency." It is not doubt
as to which to choose to do.

There is one other passage in the *Analects* that is of particular interest in connection with choice. More than any other
passage, this one seems to me to present a situation where the
issue, as we would define it, is one of internal conflict in the
moral code, a conflict to be resolved by personal choice. We are
told (13:18) of a man called "Upright" Kung whose father stole
a sheep. Kung testified against his father. The Duke, who
reports the case to Confucius, is proud of what he considers
to be Kung's uprightness. But Confucius disagrees tactfully,
remarking that in his country the son who would protect his
father is the one who is considered upright.

The passage could be a model one for posing the need for
choice between two conflicting moral requirements. A Westerner would almost inevitably elaborate on it by emphasizing
that in this case we do have knowledge (it is right to respect
the law; it is right to protect one's parents; both are profound
obligations), but when two profound duties conflict, *we* must
choose. And it is in this necessity to make a critical choice that
lies the seed of tragedy, of responsibility, of guilt and remorse.
But this way of seeing the matter, so obvious a possibility to
us, is not even suggested by Confucius. It is the very obviousness of this view of the matter that makes Confucius's failure
to show any recognition of it the more blatant. We could have
no better proof than this that the problem of genuine choice
among real alternatives never occurred to Confucius, or at
least never clearly occurred to him as a fundamental moral
task. Confucius merely announces the way *he* sees the matter,
putting it tactfully by saying it is the custom in Li. There is
nothing to suggest a decisional problem; everything suggests
that there is a defect of knowledge, a simple error of moral
judgment on the Duke's part.

We are supported in the view that Confucius saw nothing

distinctive in this sort of situation, i.e., the sort of situation that we see as distinctively posing a choice, by the fact that in all the *Analects* there is mentioned only one such case. We know there must have been many such situations in the actual daily life of the Chinese of those times—times of exceptionally great social turmoil and transformations. Furthermore, when we take into account Confucius's stature as a moralist and his insightfulness into human nature, his failure to see or to mention the problem of internal moral conflict in such a case as this can only be accounted for by supposing that his interests, ideas, concerns, in short his entire moral and intellectual orientation, was in another direction.

Any task that is as conceivable as that of *choosing* can also be formulated, instead, in terms of the Confucian task. This is the task of objectively classifying the *prima facie* alternative paths within the order of *li*, of discovering which is the true Path and of detecting which is only an apparent path, perhaps a clearing in the brush leading nowhere except into brambles. We need only make the tacit assumption that there *is* a Way, a self-consistent, self-authenticating way of universal scope.

The notion of choice as a central feature of man's existence is only one element in a closely related complex of notions, and the absence of such a concept of choice reflects the absence of the rest of this complex. Among the chief notions closely linked to choice are moral responsibility, guilt, deserved (retributive) punishment and repentance.

Sometimes when we speak of a person as responsible for something, we refer merely to his role as a critical causal factor in bringing it about. The problem of meaning here is complex, but the general drift in this usage is to treat responsibility as a matter of production or causality rather than moral obligation.

This causal notion of responsibility is quite familiar to the ancient Chinese. There is no lack of explicit discussion of the question who or what brought about a certain state of affairs. But of course it is not discussed under a heading translatable as "responsibility." For the root sense of the latter term is the moral one, and its use with respect to mere causality is a de-moralized derivative use. The root of "responsible" is of course not "cause" or "produce" but "respond"; the root question is: Who must respond for the way things go? One who is obligated to respond for the way things go will have some actual or potential causal connection with the way things go, but not everyone who has a causal connection with the way things go is obligated to respond for how they do.

The intense concern of Confucius that a person should carry out his duties and act according to what is right reflects one aspect of our notion of responsibility. But if this were all that was characteristic of our notion of responsibility, it would be a redundancy—another way of saying that one should carry out one's duties and act rightly. What gives distinct content to the idea of responsibility is derived from the root "response." Herein lies the peculiarly personal commitment—*I* answer for this deed; it is mine—and this in turn links the notion of (moral) responsibility to those of guilt, deserved punishment and repentance. It is the one who must respond whose response may involve guilt, acceptance of punishment, repentance, restitution or merit, pride, reward.

The issues in the West can become confused because of a certain sort of utilitarian view to the effect that responsibility is ultimately a purely causal notion. On this view, "responsibility" ought to be considered merely as a matter of diagnosing past causes in order to influence future events; sanctions and reward are assignable anywhere in the human causal chain that promises future prevention. If present sanctions will deter future malfeasance, then they are justified; if sanctions will not deter, or if in a particular case they would increase tendencies to malfeasance, then countersanctions are indicated. The ground for and value of repentance lie entirely in the future deterrent consequences of repentance, not in any relation to the moral aspect of the past deed. Such value as guilt-feelings have must on this view be justified by an analogous rationale. Subtler and more complex forms of utilitarian views have been emphasized in recent philosophical discussion, but these do not eliminate the possibility of the type of confusion so evidently generated by the simpler view. The fact that Confucius uses language that pertains to sanctions for law-breaking has led translators to render this as "punishment" and naturally misleads the unalerted reader to suppose that Confucius understood and used our concept of punishment (with its root implication of moral guilt).

The view that never appears in Confucius, the view that is peculiar to the Graeco-Hebraic-Christian tradition and for the most part profoundly contrasting with utilitarianism, is that punishment is justified not simply by its consequences but because it is *deserved* by virtue of what went before. Punishment is an appropriate moral response to prior guilty wrongdoing by a morally responsible agent. Repentance, in turn, is not simply a device which is appropriate or not depending on *its* psychological consequences; it is repentance *for* the past deed. Repentance is a moral response to a past wrongdoing for which one is morally responsible. Guilt is a moral (or spiritual) property accruing by virtue of accomplished wrong.

If punishment is given and received as a genuine moral experience, it is a kind of payment of a moral debt—a clearing of the slate. Of course a person may as a consequence also be inclined to be more averse to similar future wrongdoing, to the guilt-feeling it involves as well as to the quite nonmoral discomfort and the pain of the punishment. And if repentance is genuine, it constitutes an expression of repugnance with oneself for one's former course of conduct, an acknowledgment of moral guilt, and therefore it is expressed in a recommitment to a different course in the future. Thus normally the *consequences* of guilt, punishment and repentance upon moral character and upon morality-related behavior are likely to be salutary. There is a utilitarian value here. But the moral *ground* for each, that which gives it its moral status, is the past wrongdoing for which one was (morally) responsible. Were "punishment," "guilt" and "repentance" to be unrelated to prior moral wrong for which the person was responsible, we would have social engineering rather than morality—and this was precisely why Confucius took the use of "punishments" as a main target and saw his own positive teaching as in direct contrast.

For Confucius moral education consists in learning the codes of *li,* in studying literature, music and the civilizing arts in general. One's own effort provides the "push," but it is the intrinsic nobility of the goal that provides the "pull." It is by *being* a spiritually noble man that the teacher—or Prince— draws others into the direction of the Way. It is the Way that has power, and this power is effortless, invisible, magical. It is characteristic of the *Analects* that in every case, except for one clearly late "Legalist" insertion (13:3), the use of sanctions and punishment is explicitly contrasted as the undesirable alternative to the use of virtue *(te),* of humaneness *(jen),* of ceremonial propriety *(li)* and of such related strategies as "yielding" *(jang).* The *Analects* present the issue flatly: either one can govern by *li* and "yielding" or one can't (4:13); if one can't, then there is no use deceiving ourselves, and we might as well turn to "punishment," to sanctions and rewards. For these can influence people in a coercive way or by payment; but they are not truly human (i.e., moral) ways, nor do they establish a truly human life. Lacking any concept of moral guilt, or of moral responsibility as the ground for guilt and hence punishment as *moral* retribution, Confucius could see no humane potentiality in the use of sanctions.

We should not suppose that the contrary, pro-"utilitarian" point of view on these issues was alien to the Chinese mind of the times rather than being a view whose rejection by Confucius was distinctive of his own viewpoint. Confucius's outlook was in obvious contrast to that of a rival group which soon became very powerful, the so-called Legalists. Typically the latter taught that reliance on anything but the stick or the carrot was sentimental self-deception. They thought the moral approach a sham and ultimately a snare for the user.

For the tiger is able to subdue the dog because of its claws and fangs. If the tiger abandons its claws and fangs and lets the dog use them, it will be subdued by the dog. Similarly, the ruler controls his ministers through punishment and kindness (i.e., the "advantages" of "congratulations and rewards").[1]

This Legalist text contrasts flatly with the Confucian teaching: the Master said, govern the people by regulations, keep order among them by punishments, and they will evade shamelessly. Govern them by moral force (te), keep order among them by ritual (li), and there will be not only shame but correctness (2:3).

There is tacit agreement, however, that punishment, if it has any role at all, has the purely utilitarian role of practical deterrent and not of moral desert. More to the point: the notion of punishment as moral desert does not even arise in either the Analects or Legalist thought. We must, therefore, avoid reading moral meaning into the term here.

Furthermore, as has been suggested already—and it now calls for more detailed comment—there is developed in the Analects no notion of guilt and repentance as a moral response to one's wrongdoing. It is recognized that one may regret for practical reasons one's previous actions; one may change

1. Han Fei Tzu (circa 250 B.C.), cited in Chan, Source Book, p. 256.

course and follow the Way. But the "inward" stain of guilt is absent. It will, as usual, repay us to consider in a little detail some apparent exceptions to this thesis, not merely in order to support the thesis but to see better how to read the text rather than reading our own ideas into the text.

One group of passages in the *Analects* deals with "shame" *(ch'ih)*, another group deals with inner flaws; a final passage seems to call for inward self-accusation. All of these, therefore, at least suggest a quasi-explicit concern with moral responsibility and guilt-related notions.

One reference to shame *(ch'ih)* has already been cited: where one relies on punishment (i.e., fear), there is no shame; where one relies on *te*, there is shame. (2:3) *Te* may be rendered as the power of virtue, or as the virtue of one who is *jen* and follows *li;* it is the power or virtue inherent in the Way. It is to be contrasted with physical or coercive power. Thus the passage cited, as well as others, makes it clear that shame is conceived by Confucius as a moral response. And this raises the question whether the term *ch'ih* really amounts to "guilt" rather than "shame." *Ch'ih* is certainly the closest that Confucius comes to mentioning anything like guilt. The word, therefore, calls for careful examination.

The notion *ch'ih* occurs in several contexts. One group of remarks deals with the concern for or the possession of material advantages for themselves alone—e.g., good clothes, good food, wealth. [4:9; 8:13(3); 9:26(1); 14:1] These, when acquired by departing from the Way, deserve *ch'ih*. Another group of comments concerns one's public commitments and *ch'ih* from the failure to keep them. [4:22; 14:29(1)] Another group concerns *ch'ih* deserved for excess in speech, appearance, obsequiousness, pride and dissembling. [4:22; 5:14; 5:24; 14:29(1)] Finally, and more generally, *ch'ih* is a specifically moral response several times paired with disgrace *(ju)*, and in these contexts it seems to be the analogue in private conduct of the public officer's acting with disgrace in his official role. (1:13; 13:20)

If we are unaware of the crucial differences in perspective, these texts on *ch'ih* lend themselves easily to an assimilation of Confucian "shame" with Western "guilt." Yet the differences are crucial with respect to the issues that concern us here. Although *ch'ih* is definitely a moral concept and designates a moral condition or response, the moral relation to which it corresponds is that of the person to his status and role as defined by *li. Ch'ih* thus looks "outward," not "inward." It is a matter of the spoken but empty word, of the immorally gained material possession, of the excessive in appearance and in conduct. It is not, as is guilt, a matter of the inward state, of repugnance at inner corruption, of self-denigration, of the sense that one is as a person, and independently of one's public status and repute, mean or reprehensible.

It would be a basic error, however, to assume that shame is concerned with "mere appearances" rather than moral realities. The Confucian concept of shame is a genuinely moral concept, but it is oriented to morality as centering in *li*, traditionally ceremonially defined social comportment, rather than to an inner core of one's being, "the self." The violation of the moral order is thus of the essence in Confucian shame no less than in Western guilt. A personal response, a morally infused feeling-tone is also crucial in both cases. But the direction in which one turns to interpret and to deal with this feeling is different in the two cases. True, the ground for guilt is some immoral act or betrayal of someone other than oneself, but the object of guilt is oneself. Ultimately, guilt is an attack upon oneself, whereas shame is an attack upon some specific action or outer condition. Shame is a matter of "face," of embarrassment, of social status. Shame says, "change your ways; you have lost honor or dignity." Guilt says, "change yourself; you are infected." A St. Augustine can speak of the "disease of my soul," of its "wound," of "sticking in the mire," of being plucked out of the mire and washed by God, of being soul-sick and monstrous. It takes no demonstration to remind even the casual reader of Confucius that such imagery, or analogous tone, is alien to the *Analects*.

There are two passages in the *Analects* that suggest moral corruption, which at first glance might be thought akin, say, to the corruption contemplated by Augustine. One passage is about Tsai Yu. (5:9) In this passage, how different in import from Orphic, Hebrew or Christian imagery is the imagery of Confucius. Tsai Yu is rotten wood which cannot be carved, a wall of dried dung which cannot be troweled, a man who sleeps all day. Here the active disease, the fulminating wound of Augustine, is replaced by a state of mere deadness, of passivity and inherent insensitivity to moral values. Tsai Yu is at the utmost stage of the loss of capacity to be a moral human being. But in Augustine's imagery, the intensity and dynamism of the corrupting guilt are the measure of the *vitality* of his moral concern and of his imminent conversion.

The second statement in the *Analects* about moral corruption does suggest inner sickness; it is to the effect that a man would naturally have no anxiety or fear if he looked within and found nothing ill (sick). [12:4(3)] But this is the single such use of the image of "illness." We can, I believe, treat this isolated comment about "illness" as an *ad hoc*, unelaborated metaphor, one which, unlike a number of others, receives no further sign of interest on Confucius's part. It certainly is not an enunciation or metaphor of a central doctrine. Its precise point remains therefore obscure, though we are not likely to feel this because the image is so familiar to us and has so rich a meaning for us in *our* usage.

There remain two other passages that call for comment here since they do explicitly call for an orientation "inward" and for "self-accusation." Confucius in one passage enjoins us to look "in" ourselves when we see others who are not worthy. (4:17) In another place he bemoans the fact that no one is able to see his own transgressions and bring charges "within" himself. (5:26) Once again, our own rich background imagery of the inner life seems to make these passages stand as simple and plain evidence of Confucius's appreciation of the inner world of the self, of guilt or, as Legge suggests,[2] of conscience and of moral responsibility.

Perhaps the recognition that, together with the "inner ill" of 12:4(3), we find in the entire text of the *Analects* a total of only three such "inward-looking" comments ought to remind us to be more cautious in supposing that Confucius was talking of conscience and guilt. For if conscience or guilt are clearly appreciated at all, it must be clear that they are central to the moral life of most men. Why, if Confucius had in mind notions presupposing and stressing an "inner" life, should there be only three such references out of some 500 paragraphs (a number of which, in turn, treat more than one topic)? And why should these few references be so vague and unelaborated? We know that Confucius did not hesitate to repeat and to elaborate other notions such as *Tao, jen, te, li;* and the *Analects* as a whole and in all its detail is predominantly moralizing discourse, the kind that above all others invites elaboration of the themes of conscience, guilt and the inner life.

In fact these last two comments using the "look inward" image may be read in quite other contexts completely consistent with his main emphases. The comment in 4:17 tells us to concern ourselves with being like men who are worthy. But what of those men we meet who are not? The natural inclination in an age, like Confucius's of political in-fighting, social competition, military combat and contentious litigation, would be to seize upon the other's flaws, to hold them up to

2. See Legge, *Confucian Analects*, p. 183, note 26.

the light, to relish doing so and to profit from them. Confucius admonishes us instead to look "in ourself" (4:17), to "bring charges in ourself." (5:26) The former comment is entirely vague and unelaborated. The latter saying may well have been uttered in the specific, and at the time, very common context where public accusation and litigation were being explicitly discussed. Quite naturally in such a context Confucius says, in effect, don't look for the splinter in the other fellow's eye; better to discover the beam in one's own. In its juristic imagery, Confucius's comment in 5:26 is also similar to Jesus' "judge not." But whereas the language of accusation, trial and judgment pervades both Old and New Testament, it occurs as a moral metaphor only this once in the entire *Analects*. We in the West know all too well the aptness of this metaphor, too, for the moral life; therefore, from its being used and thereafter ignored, I believe we must draw, once again, the inference that Confucius was systematically oriented in another direction and saw only an *ad hoc*, topical reference in the metaphor.

There are more positive grounds for taking this "self-accusation" to be an *ad hoc* metaphor on Confucius's part, a metaphor incompatible with his main orientation and used only in a special context for special purposes. Not only is the whole spirit of the *Analects against* litigation (punishments, regulations, etc.) but Confucius says explicitly that "what is necessary is that there be no litigation." (12:13) The standard use of the word "*sung*" to mean litigation rather than a moral stance, the negative attitude toward litigation, and the single use of it with a moral nuance in this one passage suggest strongly that this emphatically exclamatory sentence is to be taken in an ironic sense: people today are constantly squabbling with each other, instituting charges against the real and fancied misdeeds of others—"If they are so quick to bring charges, why is it that I've yet to see anyone who could see his own misdeed and bring the charge to himself!" (5:26)

In the preceding commentary on the text, I have considered the possibility that Confucius does concern himself in substance with choice, responsibility, punishment as moral desert, guilt and repentance. The conclusions reached may be summarized as follows. Although the opportunity for explicitly and richly elaborating the notion of choice is latent in the central imagery of the Path, that opportunity is with remarkable thoroughness ignored. And, although there are isolated references to a moral illness, self-accusations, and inner examination—each potentially so fertile and apt for use by one concerned with responsibility, guilt and repentance—none of these is developed or in any way further remarked upon by Confucius. They remain isolated, *ad hoc* metaphors, very possibly with an ironic or topical meaning in their original context, a meaning now lost in the cryptic saying handed down to us. Finally, although there is more frequent and systematic reference to shame, this is associated with specific external possessions, conduct or status; it is a moral sentiment focused upon one's status and conduct in relation to the world rather than an inward charge against one's stained, corrupt self. The absence of the choice-responsibility-guilt complex of concepts, taken in the textual context, warrants the inference in connection with such an insightful philosopher of human nature and morality, that the concepts in question and their related imagery, were not rejected by Confucius but rather were simply not present in his thinking at all.

The language and imagery that *is* elaborated and that forms the main frame of Confucius's thought presents a different but intelligible and harmonious picture to us. Man is not an ultimately autonomous being who has an inner and decisive power, intrinsic to him, a power to select among real alternatives and thereby to shape a life for himself. Instead he is born as "raw material" who must be civilized by education and thus become a truly human man. To do this he must aim at the

Way, and the Way must—through its nobility and the nobility of those who pursue it—attract him. This outcome is not conceived as one that enhances a personal power as over against society or the physical environment, but rather as one that sharpens and steadies a person's "aim" or orientation to the point where he can undeviatingly walk the one true Way: he is a civilized human being. Walking the Way incarnates in him the vast spiritual dignity and power that reside in the Way. One who walks the Way rather than going astray, who does so "naturally," "yielding" rather than forcing, such a man lives a life of personal dignity and fulfillment, of social harmony with others based on mutual respect allowing to each just such a life.

Therefore the central moral issue for Confucius is not the responsibility of a man for deeds he has by his own free will chosen to perform, but the factual questions of whether a man is properly taught the Way and whether he has the desire to learn diligently. The proper response to a failure to conform to the moral order *(li)* is not self-condemnation for a free and responsible, though evil, choice, but self-reeducation to overcome a mere defect, a lack of power, in short a lack in one's "formation." The Westerner's inclination to press at this point the issue of personal responsibility for lack of diligence is precisely the sort of issue that is never even raised in the *Analects.*

To summarize finally in a schematic way, moral problems resolve into one of four forms for Confucius: (1) the wrongdoer is not well enough educated to be able to recognize and properly classify what is according to the Way and what is not; (2) the wrongdoer has not yet learned the requisite skills to follow the Way in some respect; (3) the wrongdoer has not *persisted* in the required effort (this is conceived as a matter of strength, not choice); (4) the wrongdoer knows enough to go through some of the motions, but he is not totally committed to the

Way, and he is then either erratic or he systematically perverts the outer forms of *li* to serve personal profit.

Confucius's vision provides no basis for seeing man as a being of tragedy, of inner crisis and guilt; but it does provide a socially oriented, action-oriented view which provides for personal dignity. Moreover, when we place the comments made here in the larger context of Confucius's view of man, a context further discussed in the other essays in this book, we see then that the images of the inner man and of his inner conflict are not essential to a concept of man as a being whose dignity is the consummation of a life of subtlety and sophistication, a life in which human conduct can be intelligible in natural terms and yet be attuned to the sacred, a life in which the practical, the intellectual and the spiritual are equally revered and are harmonized in the one act—the act of *li*.

3

The Locus
of the Personal

There is no doubt that for Confucius *"jen"* is at least equal
in importance to any other single concept such as *li*. Unlike
li, however, *jen* is surrounded with paradox and mystery in
the *Analects. Jen* seems to emphasize the individual, the subjective, the character, feelings and attitudes; it seems, in short, a
psychological notion. The problem of interpreting *jen* thus
becomes particularly acute if one thinks, as I do, that it is of
the essence of the *Analects* that the thought expressed in it is
not based on psychological notions. And, indeed, one of the
chief results of the present analysis of *jen* will be to reveal how
Confucius could handle in a nonpsychological way basic issues
which we in the West naturally cast in psychological terms.
The psychological, subjective use of *jen* in Chinese is a later
development, a use whose import is exaggerated both by the
profound psychological bias of Buddhist commentators and
by the Western, Graeco-Christian outlook of translators. The
truly novel aspects of Confucius's doctrine of *jen* are precisely
what we need to see but fail to see because they *are* novel and
hence not easily formulated in the psychologically biased language we have ready to hand.

Jen has been translated variously as Good, Humanity, Love,
Benevolence, Virtue, Manhood, Manhood-at-Its-Best and so
on. For various commentators *jen* has seemed to be a virtue,

the all-inclusive virtue, a spiritual condition, a complex of attitude and feelings, a mystic entity. Its relation to *li* and to other important concepts remains obscure. Let us see if we can propose a meaning that will articulate precisely and clearly with the main ideas in the *Analects*. A further test will be whether our account of its meaning will substantiate Confucius's words: "There is nothing that I keep from you." But we must now turn to the task of developing afresh the interpretation of *jen*.

Waley says that *jen* is a "mystic entity."[1] There is no doubt that at least on the face of the text there is paradox. We are told *jen* is itself a heavy burden:

The True Knight of the Way must be great and strong; his burden is heavy, and his course is long. He has taken *jen* as his burden—is that not heavy? Only with death does his journey end—is that not long? (8:7)

But we are also told that *jen* comes "*after* what is difficult is duly done." (6:20)

And finally we seem to be told that it is neither difficult nor need wait till after the difficult is done: "Is *jen* so far away? I desire it, and lo!—it is here." (7:29)

Of one thing there is no doubt: *jen* is central to the ideal life. For example, Confucius says that:

One who really cared for *jen* would not let any other consideration come first. (4:6)

(An alternative but equally emphatic translation is: "One who really cared for *jen* would be surpassed by no one."[2])

What are the observable and characteristic traits of a *jen* man? Here, too, we are initially puzzled. Not only are we told that, in general, Confucius "rarely spoke of profit, fate, or *jen*,"

---

1. Waley, *Analects of Confucius*, p. 28.
2. Chan, *Source Book*, p. 26, note 55.

(9:1),[3] but he seems to say that the *jen* man is chary of speaking about it. (12:3)[4] Yet we cannot suppose that this latter comment provides a clear direction which we can follow, for no one seems to be able to find a formula, acceptable to Confucius, for identifying actual men who are or were *jen*. Indeed if we turn to those books of the *Analects* which are generally acknowledged to be the earliest "strata," the most authentically direct reports of Confucius's words, there is extremely little about what *jen* itself is. The comments fall into several main groupings.

In Books 2 through 9, and more spottily in 11 through 15, a good deal of the comment is negative, a series of rejections of suggestions of various commendable actions as necessarily signs of *jen*. (5:4, 7, 18; 7:33; 14:2, 17)

There is another group of passages which consist of general comments about the struggle for *jen*. Thus, as we have noted, it comes before any other consideration (4:6); the noble man never abandons it even for a moment. (4:5) It comes only after one has done what is difficult. (6:20) Yet it is not a question of insufficient strength but the will to use all one's strength. (4:6) One may have to give one's life for *jen*. (15:8)

3. In spite of the controversy over the reading of this passage, I think the traditional one, also concurred in by Waley, *Analects of Confucius* (p. 29), is correct. It makes sense to me from a philosophical standpoint. In addition, and in spite of Bodde's and Laufer's arguments, it seems to me to be justified, or at least rendered an open question, on stylistic grounds. Bodde argues that in these chain phrasings the conjunction *yu* is never used elsewhere in the *Analects*. But what he does not mention is that in such a closely neighboring passage as 9:4, we find almost a mirror-image of 9:1 except that the negative *mu* is used instead of the affirmative *yu* of 9:1. Why should not a sense of parallelism and rhythm have called for this perfectly permissible use of *yu* instead of the more common omission of any explicit conjunction?
4. Here again the reading is controversial. I have followed Waley, *Analects of Confucius* (p. 163, note 2), rather than most other translators. The ambiguity of *chih* after *wei* and *yen* allows either that the *jen* man is chary of speech in general or of speaking about *jen* in particular. Given the option, I have decided on philosophical grounds of the kind indicated in the argument that is presented in my exposition.

Many other comments about *jen* are also quite general but concern the consequences and great power of *jen*. Without *jen*, a man cannot for long endure either adversity or prosperity. (4:2) Those who are *jen* rest content in *jen*; those who are wise profit from it. (4:2)

The power of jen is expressed—but with some ambiguity—in the statement that if one submits to *li*, everyone will respond to one's *jen*. (12:1) If a truly Kingly Man were to arise, within a single generation *jen* would prevail. (13:12) In each of the latter cases, the power of *jen* is explicitly linked to other conditions, kingliness or submission to *li*.

One passage seems to say that only the *jen* know how to love men and how to hate them (4:3), whereas those who sincerely strive to become *jen* abstain from hatred. (4:4) The text is obscure on this latter point, and Waley renders the passage so as to give an essentially opposite meaning. When opposite interpretations can be given to a passage on such a central question, it becomes all too evident that the concept *jen* is obscure.

In spite of all these comments on *jen*, there is a point to the saying that the Master "never spoke of *jen*," for the comments we have examined really tell us very little, if anything, of what *jen* is *in itself*. Yet we should not suppose that something is being hidden from us: The Master said: "My friends, I know you think that there is something I am keeping from you. There is nothing that I keep from you. I do nothing which you do not know." (7:23) We must take this disclaimer in all seriousness. Waley has suggested that Confucius is talking here only about his actions *(hsing)* and not necessarily about esoteric doctrine. But, as I argue here and in the other essays in this book, Confucius speaks in terms of action *(hsing)* because for him it is action and public circumstances that are fundamental, not esoteric doctrine or subjective states. We can at least provisionally dismiss this complex question by again quoting the Master:[5] the noble man "first declares himself, then follows through." (2:13)

Is there nothing we can learn from the Master regarding *jen* itself, its positive nature, the definition of the term or at least some definite traits of the *jen* man? There are a few clues, though one cannot help noting that the most explicit of these are, as one might expect, in the later or in any case less certainly authentic remarks of Confucius.

I shall pass lightly over certain rather cliché virtues ascribed in the later books to those who are *jen*. "Courteous," "diligent," "loyal," "brave," "broad," "kind" (13:19; 14:5; 17:6)—these are traditional virtues which give us no insight or other help. Furthermore, aside from the questionable authenticity of these later passages, especially 17:6, they are not decisive since, as we noted earlier, Confucius at various times indicates that the possession of such virtues is not sufficient for establishing that a man is *jen*. (Cf. 5:18; 5:7; 14:2; 14:5)

A distinctive but suspect pattern of characterization is reflected in a series of comments, most of which, however, come from 6:21. The latter text, as Waley points out,[6] looks suspiciously Taoist and probably is corrupt. It tells us that the man who is *jen* is content to be *jen*; while knowledge keeps one on the move, the man of *jen* delights in mountains (6:21), and he is tranquil (6:21) and long-lived (6:21).

We now turn to some of the most specific and most helpful comments about the nature of *jen* itself.

You want to be established yourself, then seek to establish others. You wish to advance, then advance others. From what is near to one to seize the analogy (i.e., to take one's neighbor as oneself) — there is *jen's* way. (6:28)[7]

5. See also, for example: 2:10; 5:9.
6. Waley: see especially pp. 239–40.
7. The version in parentheses is my attempt to render the meaning of an admittedly obscure phrase by retaining, but also making more explicit the key

He who can submit himself to *li* is *jen*. (12:1)

In both the preceding comments, *jen* is intimately linked to the relationship between man and man. In the first instance, this link is to the general reciprocal good faith and respect among men *(shu* and *chung)*; in the second instance this reciprocal good faith is given a specific content: it is that set of specific social relationships articulated in detail by *li*. In short, where reciprocal good faith and respect are expressed through the specific forms defined in *li*, there is *jen's* way.

Thus *li* and *jen* are two aspects of the same thing. Each points to an aspect of the action of man in his distinctively human role. *Li* directs our attention to the traditional social pattern of conduct and relationships; *jen* directs our attention to the person as the one who pursues that pattern of conduct and thus maintains those relationships. *Li* also refers to the particular act in its status as exemplification of invariant norm; *jen* refers to the act as expressive of an orientation of the person, as expressing his commitment to act as prescribed by *li*. *Li* refers to the act as overt and distinguishable pattern of sequential behavior; *jen* refers to the act as the single, indivisible gesture of an actor, as his, and as particular and individual by reference to the unique individual who performs the act

---

metaphors of "grasping" and "near." I have tried to bring out explicitly what I take to be the terms of the "analogy," and I have tried to use words very close in meaning or etymology to those we might use in a more "literal" translation. As for the phrase *"jen's* way," because it seems not only concise and stylistically appropriate but because it is the only such concise phrase I can think of that retains the same ambiguity to be found in the original. This cryptic phrase follows a cryptic formula which in turn follows a more elaborate and plainer formula. But what precisely are the logical connections among these formulas? Are they variant definitions of *jen?* Are they different formulations of a way of getting to be *jen* (rather than descriptions of how one acts when one is *jen*)? Is one a method of getting there and the other a definition of *jen* or a localization of the region in which *jen* is found? Our phrase, "Smith's way," allows all of these meanings when unrestricted by context: (1) the way of getting to Smith's, (2) the immediate region where Smith lives, and (3) the way of action that is characteristic of Smith.

and to the unique context of the particular action.

Our more familiar Western terminology would be misleading. We are tempted to go further than I have above and to say *jen* refers to the attitudes, feelings, wishes and will. This terminology is misleading. The thing we must *not* do is to psychologize Confucius's terminology in the *Analects*. The first step in seeing that this is so is to recognize that *jen* and its associated "virtues," and *li* too, are not connected in the original text with the language of "will," "emotion" and "inner states." The move from *jen* as referring us to a person on to *jen* as "therefore" referring us to his inner mental or psychic condition or processes finds no parallel in the *Analects*. Certainly there is no systematic or even unsystematic elaboration of any such connections.

The only apparent exception to the above thesis is to be found in 9:28 and repeated in 14:30. Here, in both passages, we are told that the *jen* man is not *yu* (roughly: unhappy, anxious, troubled). What is more, the context suggests that this is not an incidental, but rather an essential characterization. Because of this apparently inner, subjective reference, and because of the suggestion that we deal here with something central to *jen*, we shall turn to a closer examination of these key passages and of the term *yu*.

In both passages we have a plainly rhythmic parallelism of internal structure. Three central virtues are mentioned, and in the same syntactical formula each virtue is characterized in a single phrase in the negative. The wise are not perplexed; the brave are not fearful; the *jen* are not *yu*. The almost tautological character of the first two phrases suggest that we should take in a similar way "the *jen* are not *yu*." *Yu*, it is fair to presume, is the opposite of *jen*.

A careful consideration of the meaning of *yu*, therefore, seems to be called for here. It will provide us with a deeper understanding—and corroboration—of the thesis of this discussion.

If we turn to the other passages in the *Analects* where *yu* is used, we find that the translations vary from translator to translator for any passage, and they vary from passage to passage for the same translator. Where Legge translates "sorrow," Waley translates "trouble," Leslie translates into French *"regretter,"* and also *"embarras."* (16:1-8, 13) Or again, the term as used in 7:18 is translated "sorrows" (Legge), "bitterness" (Waley), "worries" (Chan), *"chagrins"* (Leslie). The pattern is repeated again and again: clearly the translators are choosing what they take to be an appropriate specific European term for a Chinese term which does not completely coincide.

If we look to see whether there is a common denominator to all these uses, we certainly find that in all uses *yu* implies a troubled condition. The word "troubled" implies both "unsettled," "untranquil," "disturbed" and also "with ominous and unpleasant significance uppermost." Translations such as "sorrow," "worry" and "bitterness" place the stress on what we would call the subjective state, the emotions and feelings of the person. This is a natural approach for a Westerner. The consequence is that, if the *jen* man is more or less equivalent to the man who is not *yu*, then *jen* is a psychological term since it would seem to be the contrary of *yu*.

However an examination of the actual texts, which provide the context of the use of *yu*, presents a different picture. In 2:6 the parents are *yu* about the child's illness. Here we have the parents characterized by reference to objective and ominous trouble, to objective unsettledness in the situation. Their response to trouble is a troubled response. The Westerner readily and naturally locates the "trouble" of the response in an "internal" psychic condition. But we must force ourself to look at the text here and see that, at least in this passage, there is no language of the psychically internal or subjective. The child's illness is an observable condition, and so, one may truly say, is the troubled response of the parents. Not the text, but our own tacit presuppositions lead to supposing that the parents' troubledness is necessarily to be conceived as rooted in troubled "inner" states.

In 7:3 Confucius announces that the failure to pursue man's virtue *(te)*, learning, morality—these make him *yu*. Again we find the person's response is in objective disorder and confusion, for these are the Confucian contraries of the Confucian way: they are *misconduct*. In 7:18 Confucius speaks of himself as so joyful and eager in pursuit of enlightenment that he forgets *yu* and that old age is coming on. Here again, the ominous but quite objective uncertainties of old age are side by side with *yu*.

I must emphasize that my point here is not that Confucius's words are intended to exclude reference to the inner psyche. He could have done this if he had had such a basic metaphor in mind, had seen its plausibility, but on reflection had decided to reject it. But this is not what I am arguing here. My thesis is that the entire notion never entered his head. The metaphor of an inner psychic life, in all its ramifications so familiar to us, simply isn't present in the *Analects*, not even as a rejected possibility. Hence when I say that in the above passages using *yu* there is no reference to the inner, subjective states, I do not mean that these passages clearly and explicitly exclude such elaboration, but that they make no use of it and do not require it for intelligibility or validity.

In 12:4 we find the closest to a "psychological" use of *yu* in the *Analects*. The noble man is neither *yu* nor afraid. Why? Because when he "looks within" he finds no "sickness." The image of looking "within" suggests—to us—a notion of the "inner life." But we must not fail to notice that *what* we are looking for is not presented as a "subjective state" but as "sickness." No doubt Confucius means something like "moral sickness" or "spiritual sickness." No doubt one of the chief achievements of Confucius was to see and to teach, in a way none before him in China had, that there is a spiritual-moral dimension of human existence. But the point at issue is whether he systematically located this spiritual dimension "inside" the individual. Since we of the West can hardly conceive of it except in the language and imagery of the "inner," the first important step in learning what Confucius can teach us on this topic is at least to notice that, although occasion for use of such language is ever present in the *Analects*, its absence is (from our standpoint) glaring. To anticipate, I will merely remark here that for Confucius, the spiritual is public, "outer" —but not in the sense that it is embodied in gods or other nonhuman beings or nonhuman powers.

The text does reveal that he on at least three occasions vaguely alluded to the "inside," but on the other hand he constantly talked, in elaborated terms, of conduct, comportment and the rules of conduct. What is more, his references to the "inside" and to the "private" are always by way of locating here one source of sickness, lack of moral development. Success, the positive characterization of moral development, is always a matter of objective comportment—of the reciprocal good faith and respect expressed specifically and concretely in *li*.

In a further series of uses of *yu* (12:5, 15:11, 15:31), we learn that without brothers (i.e., family), one is *yu*, and with respect to the future the wise person is *yu*—and naturally enough, for here are two of the chief conditions of objective uncertainty and potential danger. We also learn that the noble man is *yu* with regard to the *Tao*, but not *yu* with regard to poverty. Here again, the notion of objective uncertainty and unsettledness with possible ominous import is relevant. The noble man is not on the road to wealth; hence any uncertainty about it imports no troubled unsettledness in his comportment. But it is quite otherwise with regard to the *Tao*. Here all is risked, and the Way is not easy. Only the Sage is able to walk the Way in a completely stable, spontaneous way.

Even in the obviously much later passage of 16:1, the word *yu* is still used in what is clearly the context of an objectively troubled state, one associated with military and political troubles.

In summary, then, the condition of being *yu*, whose absence is critically characteristic of the *jen* man, is the condition of a person involved in and responding in an objectively unsettled, troubled situation where a bad outcome is a distinct and evident possibility.

It follows that the absence of *yu* is the condition of a man who is responding in a way that is well integrated into an objectively settled and organized situation. What is this condition? Clearly we have described what, for Confucius, is the condition of a man who has "submitted to *li*." Ideally, he should live in a society that is genuinely governed by *li*.

Since *li* is that structure of human conduct that harmonizes the doings of all men and establishes their well-being as men, it is clear that he who is fully established in *li* is living a life that is perfectly organized and is entirely conducive to the flowering of human existence.

If *jen* is the aspect of conduct that directs our attention to the particular person and his orientation as the actor, it is clear that the objective failure to conform to *li* will be perceived, from the actor-perspective, as an objective, disquieting lack of clear direction or readiness in the stance of the actor; there will be disruptedness, troubledness and trouble. In short *yu* is indeed the absence of *jen*, and *jen* is the absence of *yu*.

We are now in a position to comment on, and I believe make intelligible, the paradox that *jen* is both difficult and yet is here for the wishing. And this will show further how *jen* is not a psychological concept referring to the "inner" self.

Jen requires "doing what is difficult first" because man is born with only the raw stuff of humanity: the uncarved, unpolished material, the raw impulses and potential which can be fashioned into a mature person. An organized personal stance has not yet been achieved. *Jen* develops only so far as *li* develops; it is the shaping of oneself *in li*.

For example, one cannot have a profound and intelligent loyalty toward one's prince until one has reached the stage where one has knowledge about social-political relations and problems, until one has had reasonably extensive experience in these matters, until, in short, one has learned, by participation, the specific character of governmental affairs. We must appreciate the gap between a child's naïve, simple and unsophisticated clinging and dependence, and the profound and sophisticated loyalty of a great statesman to his prince. The movement across this gap is the learning and mastery of *li*. Similarly, the love and loyalty of a husband for a wife, however intense it may be at first, is relatively amorphous and impoverished in content as compared to what it may become over the course of many years of married life through crises, good fortune and sheer routine. Ultimately, this personal stance of each toward the other cannot be cultivated, deepened and enriched, except by entering into a series of new situations requiring new forms of conduct, new obligations, new kinds of yielding and taking. Suffering (in the classical sense) and acting are what shape the man. Thus, until *li* is learned, *jen* cannot be realized. One cannot ripen without the other, since they are merely different perspectives on one and the same thing.

Jen comes "after doing what is difficult." Of course, it takes time, effort, persistence to learn *li;* and therefore it takes time, effort, and persistence before one can be *jen.*

A man who is not *jen* can have nothing to do with *li.* (3:3)

The man who can submit himself to *li* is *jen*. (12:1) It works both ways.

Jen is ready at hand for wishing. What does this mean? The answer to this is more complex; but it is also more revealing.

Li stresses the act as overt, the series of movements through space and time. As such, the act is analyzable into segments, into a series of steps, each step a prerequisite for its successor. There is therefore a *way* (i.e., a sequence of steps by which) to carry out *li*, but not so with *jen*. When we look at action from the standpoint of the actor, we use categories that do not provide us with complex patterns of action analyzable in spatial and temporal relationships but with "simple" acts. To put it another way: to look at an act from the standpoint of the actor is not to shift from outer space and time, and to look instead into an inner mysterious realm, but it is to characterize the act in terms of categories that do not have the same logical features as the ones that characterize the act as overt behavior. What does this mean in the case at hand?

One decides to greet someone and does so. The *greeting* is *li*: in a certain kind of context we observe a sequence of overt movements—the movement of hand and arm in complex sequences, the utterance of prescribed phrases, the coordinated execution of a series of actions which can be analyzed into elements, behavioral and linguistic, extending through space and time. But the *deciding* to greet the person need not be conceived as another "inner" act, a "mental" act which is also necessarily analyzable into steps consisting of mental actions. There is no inherent *way* or *method* of deciding. One simply decides. It may take time *until* we decide; that is, our deliberations may extend through time. We may upon occasion use one or another handy method to help us come to our decision. None of this is essential to the decision; it does not constitute the decision as the shaking of the person's hand is a constitutive element in that act of greeting. The point can be seen in this way: we could have made the *same* decision though our deliberations preceding it had taken a different route; but we cannot give the *same* greeting except by taking the very same steps. The steps constitute the greeting. But there are no steps that *constitute* the decision.

One may portray this to oneself as evidence of the miraculous or magical character of the act of decision, an act having no steps in time and space but just "happening" at an instant —and this is what Confucius tended to do.

Or one may portray "deciding" ("deciding to be *jen*") to oneself as a process or an act taking place in a mysterious inner, private or "mental" realm where there is supposedly invisible "machinery," "structures" or "agencies," as we of the West have so often done, especially since Descartes.

Or one may portray this type of contrast between such acts as "deciding" and "greeting" as a difference in the "logical" role of the concepts. On this view, "He decided to greet John," no more reports a mysterious act in an inner psychic realm than "He made a profit" reports an act in an economic realm that is distinct from his observable acts of buying and selling. Since the phrase "make a profit" and the phrase "make a decision" are not used to point out the sequential, spatial and bodily aspects of conduct *per se*, it is on this view no mystery of metaphysics but a truth of "grammar" that one cannot describe or show the behavioral sequence of "steps" that constitutes the act of deciding or making a profit.

If we can withdraw ourselves from the traditional mentalistic bias of the West, whether we do so *tout court* or by virtue of shifting to the sort of linguistic analysis sketched above, then we are freer to appreciate Confucius's notion of *jen* and related notions. Of course, we must not suppose that he was teaching or using the doctrines of contemporary philosophical analysis, nor as I have said, should we take him to be excluding or arguing against a mentalistic interpretation of human comportment. His formulation was his own, peculiar to him and without even tacit reference or allusion to mentalistic concepts and models.

Confucius merely observed and reported the truth of the matter; *jen* being a matter of the person's deciding to submit to *li* (once he has the objective skill to do so), there is no step-by-step analysis of *how* to be *jen*: one really wants to be *jen*, and lo!—it is so. There is only one way ultimately to decide and that way is—to decide!

Analogous considerations are relevant to other notions (which we in the West psychologize) such as "thinking," "feeling," "having an attitude" or "desiring." In the case of each such concept, there is no overt and analyzable process—one simply has or does not have an attitude, or thinks or desires. All of these are in such respects logically similar to the idea of *jen*. There is a "way" to ride a bicycle—in a certain temporal sequence one moves one's feet and leans in certain ways, and the doing of this as the bicycle rolls *is* the riding of the bicycle. But there is no "way" to desire or think. There is no *way* to see the validity of a step in logic or to act out of noble motives —in the last analysis, one does (or one doesn't), but to come to the point of doing so may involve much labor at self-development.

From this standpoint we now can see that in one sense there is, after all, a way to be *jen*; it is a necessary but not a sufficient means. *Jen* comes "after what is difficult is done," i.e., after one has mastered the skills of action required by *li*. Learning the skills of civilized intercourse is indeed difficult. It takes persistence, however, rather than supernormal strength. (4:6) On the other hand, there is no *way* to persist, no *way* of being *jen*: either one keeps at one's learning or one doesn't—that *is* persistence or lack of it; either one acts with equal concern for others as equally dignified in *li*—or one doesn't—that is being *jen* or not. From this perspective it is easy to be *jen*: simply,

be *jen*! Presuming one has mastered the skills of proper ceremonial action, either one does or does not conduct oneself
toward others "as though in the presence of an important
guest," as though "officiating at an important sacrifice," in
short as though others have the same fundamental dignity as
oneself. (12:2)

We can now see yet another way in which *li* must be
learned, but *jen* is immediately at hand if desired. When we
look at action from the perspective of its structure, as a pattern
of overt behavior, we are well aware that unavoidable obstacles may interrupt the pattern and thus frustrate the act. But
when we think of action in terms of the actor's orientation
toward others, the *direction* he gives his act, we see that here
we have a kind of infallibility, a fate distinguishable from the
ultimate fate of the overt act. The pianist aims at playing a
certain chord, but fails. Outer obstacles do not prevent the
aiming, only the success of the act. Hence, in this light we see
that there are no obstacles to *aiming*. All one need do is aim.
Again, analogously, we can often see a certain kind of *concern*
for others in an act even if the act fails due to obstacles. *Jen* is
a form of concern. Thus that concern which is *jen* is that "if
one wishes"—there are no obstacles. Hence it is precisely apt
to say of *jen*, but not of *li*, that "if you desire it, it is there."
Looked at from this standpoint, action again has a dimension
that, compared to some other aspects, is magical, miraculous
and paradoxical. Either one has a certain concern in one's
action, or not; it's up to the person *entirely*, yet there is no *way*
for him to make his act a genuinely concerned one.

The preceding comments have been primarily designed to
bring out the aspect of immediacy and infallibility of the *jen*
perspective, the personal perspective, and also in a way to
de-mystify this aspect, to recall to our awareness how familiar
is that perspective in our everyday life. A few further remarks
may be appropriate in this context to emphasize the natural-

ness and propriety of looking at the personal, *jen* aspect of conduct as "outer" or public even though personal.

We can perhaps best begin by re-emphasizing that Confucius examines the public and mundane world from a variety of public perspectives. He is, for example, concerned with the social *history* of the ceremony, which an act exemplifies—that is, with *li* as tradition. He is also concerned with the *pattern of overt behavior* of the act—*li* as literally a set of rules for action. He is concerned with action as *role* performance, the roles being defined by *li*—"let the prince be a prince," etc. (12:11)

And finally he is concerned with action as personal, as done by human beings and directed toward or acted jointly with other human beings—*jen*, reciprocal respect (*shu*), loyalty (*chung*), and good faith (*hsin*). How does he conceive the personal to be an objective and observable aspect of the act?

Acts that are *li* are not mere rote, formula-conforming performances; they are subtle and intelligent acts exhibiting more or less sensitivity to context, more or less integrity in performance. We would do well to take music, of which Confucius was a devotee, as our model here. We distinguish sensitive and intelligent musical performances from dull and unperceptive ones; and we detect in the performance confidence and integrity, or perhaps hesitation, conflict, "faking," "sentimentalizing." We detect all this *in* the performance; we do not have to look into the psyche or personality of the performer. It is all "there," public. Although it is there *in* the performance, it is apparent to us when we consider the performance not as "the Beethoven Opus 3" (that is, from the composer perspective), nor as a "public concert" (the *li* perspective), nor as a "post-Mozartian opus" (the style perspective), but primarily as this particular person's performance (the personal perspective).

Analogously, an act may be seen as *jen* if we look to see how *this* person does it, and more specifically whether it reveals that he treats all persons involved as of ultimately equal dignity with himself by virtue of their participation along with him in *li*. And even if the pattern of his behavior is unavoidably disrupted, we can see the direction it had, the aim, the concern *in* it, just as we can see the chord the pianist aimed to play but in the upshot failed to play. We see all this by observing the act in its observable context, not by looking into the person's head or some purely inward psychic realm.

As we can detect fakery in the musical performance, so we can on occasion observe that although an act looks like *li*, it is really an element in some more complex but dissembled act; it is aimed at enhancing the actor's own importance at the expense of the other person and in a way not sanctioned by *li*.

Let us attempt finally to place Confucius's own way of seeing *jen* in focus by putting aside a subjectivist language of intent and attitude on the one hand and a logical-linguistic analysis on the other, and try to find an image that both distinctively and truly reflects Confucius's way of seeing *jen*. Such an image must suggest a power emanating from the actor —the person who is *jen* can by means of *li* allow his power to radiate everywhere under heaven. The power must emanate from the actor, but our image must not direct our attention to the "interior" of the man but to the act of the man. Yet the image must not identify the *jen* power with the act as overt; instead, the directional, aim character of the *jen* power must be stressed as distinct from the ultimate and actual course of the act. This is to be a matter of emphasis by language and imagery, not separation of two distinct events—for the aim cannot be determined except as a feature of the behavior in the context, and the behavior cannot be understood except as interpreted in terms of some aim. Finally, this power is to be essentially *human* power; that is, it is a power of human beings (when they *are* truly human) and it is directed *toward* human beings and influences them. The Chinese of Confucius has no clear distinction between properties, qualities, definitions or essences. But we can say that *jen* is often directly associated with a *person* and suggested to be a possession of the person.

It seems to me that the Western image that would serve best is one drawn from physics—the vector. In the case of *jen*, we should conceive of a directed force operating in actions in public space and time, and having a person as initial point-source and a person as the terminal point on which the force impinges. The forces are human forces, of course, not mechanical ones.

The virtues that Confucius stresses are indeed all "dynamic" and social. For example, *shu* (mutuality in human relations), *chung* (loyalty) and *hsin* (good trust toward others)—all inherently involve a dynamic relation to other persons.[8] On the other hand, such "static" and "inner" virtues as purity or innocence play no role in the *Analects*.

We easily see *li* in terms of the imagery of an external Way, and now we can do this with *jen*. The image calls our attention to the stance, the literal stand and spatial attitude of the actor. Just as in the ceremony, we see the taking of a ritual stand and attitude as the initiating source of this particular act's power —we sense it "radiate" toward us when we are committed participants or observers at the ceremony. "(The Emperor) sat facing the South (as was ritually proper), and everything (duly) took place." The sensation of magical power which we all feel emanating from a ritual gesture (or a hypnotist's gesture)

8. *Chung* has been rendered with the sense of "being true to oneself" and also of "loyalty." The translation "true to oneself" coincides more nicely with our Western ideas or Buddhist ideas of a key virtue. But the justification for this translation cannot be found in the text of the *Analects* or even in the other early classics such as the *Shu Ching* or *I Li* (portions of which, of course, are even later than Confucius). In these contexts either there is no clear clue or else it is clear that it is loyalty and not "being true to oneself" that is in question. The only linguistic basis for the meaning "true to oneself" is the structure of the written character—"center" over "heart"—and this is at most suggestive, whereas our other evidence is plain and solid.

when made by one who is felt to be authentic in that ceremonial role—this is the way in which we should feel *jen*. And *jen* is the complete and concentrated power of the separate vectors —perfect loyalty and good faith, complete respect for human dignity and so on. Each of these, in turn, is not an inner state but a virtue in the original sense—a power emanating from the person, a vector of human power. When one has used all one's energies in learning how to master *li* and has at last accomplished this, then, as Yen Hui said, "it looms up before me." At this point there is nothing further he can draw upon in order finally to *use* the power of *jen*. (9:10) One either takes one's stand in *li* and is thus *jen*, or one does not; being able to do so, it remains only to desire to do so. But man is often afraid, at the moment of decision, to put his faith in human power; he has for so long been relying on physical force and animal force. *Jen* just *is* the perfect giving of oneself to the *human* way. It is walking to the very edge—

> In fear and trembling,
> With caution and care,
> As though on the brink of a chasm,
> As though treading thin ice. (5:3)

4

Traditionalist
or Visionary?

The Confucian ideal of *li* poses a fundamental problem. We of the twentieth century are aware of "culture conflict," aware of the conflicts of custom and value that can arise within a single culture. We, therefore, cannot help seeing a problem that Confucius never once entertains. Confucius seems to take for granted, without having questioned or even become aware of his assumptions as such, that there is one *li* and that it is in harmony with a greater, cosmic *Tao*. He assumes that this *li* is the *li* of the land in which he lives (other lands being barbarian), that the Ancients of his tradition lived this *li*. He assumes that this *li*, and the cosmic *Tao* in which it is rooted, are internally coherent and totally adequate, and that, finally, the only moral and social necessity is, therefore, to shape oneself and one's conduct in *li*. Each and every one of these interconnected and basic assumptions is initially placed in grave doubt when we take account of the now familiar fact of a plurality of great cultures each with its distinct history.

A first response to such objections to the Confucian ideal might well be that the objections are anachronistic. One could admit they apply devastatingly enough to the Confucian ideal if it is considered as a possible universal human ideal, but one could argue that the objections are anachronistic if offered as criticisms of Confucius, the fifth-century B.C. teacher from the principality of Lu. He could not have known of other great civilizations, whether of the contemporary Greek or Israelite civilizations, or of earlier ones such as the Egyptian. What the people of Lu knew was an unusually great deal about some of their own predecessors in their immediate region of Asia, and they also knew of various border tribes which clearly had no such elaborate civilization as that of Lu. Without access to additional anthropological and historical information, without any reasonable grounds for supposing such information existed, how can Confucius be legitimately criticized for supposing that there was only one great civilization, at the "center" of things, a center surrounded by border areas containing semi-civilized or barbarian peoples? How could he have reasonably entertained the possibility of other civilizations of a grandeur equal to that of his own?

A "defense" of Confucius along these lines, though legitimate as far as it goes, nevertheless pays a great price. It reduces the significance of his teaching from that of a universal, philosophical teaching to that of a historical datum. It does make it possible for us to see, as a fact of history, how his compatriots, working within similar limits of knowledge could have taken his teaching as a living option; but in the same gesture it makes it impossible to conceive of his teaching as a teaching for us. This may indeed be the upshot of the matter. Perhaps the Confucian teaching can be no more than a historical specimen to the informed citizen of the twentieth century (though my remarks in this book are designed to show precisely the contrary).

Yet there are problems that such a historical approach still leaves unsolved. The principal unsolved problem is that of the internal conflict, the intraculture conflicts. There is no question that any sophisticated resident of Confucius's time and region was all too aware of the existence of a number of different, often warring principalities. He was aware that customs differed to some extent among these peoples, differed at times very much between the small central principalities and the larger states on the periphery. Even more, a sophisticated citizen of the times could not help noticing that old ways were not infrequently being abandoned, new ways introduced. If ever there was an area beset with intracultural conflict of every kind from genteel doctrinal dispute to Machiavellian politics, plain murder and brutal warfare, surely Lu and its neighboring states were such a one. It was a time of great turmoil—including an intense *consciousness* of turmoil.

In the face of this turmoil, how could Confucius have ignored the possibility that the *li* of his land was inherently a network of often conflicting paths, a body of practices inadequate to meet the challenges of the real world? Though in the *Analects* he never raises precisely this question, he did of course teach that the turmoil was the result of moral-political degeneration through time of the original, perfect *li* of the Ancients. But the question we must raise is: *Why* should this answer appear so compelling as to prevent his ever raising the question of alternative answers? How did he arrive at *this* answer rather than one that was at least equally or (to us) even more forcefully suggested by the everyday evidence? It will not help to ascribe it to a limited imagination. We must, at least initially, presume that a thinker and a teacher of great stature has some more compelling and universal basis for the way he frames and answers his central questions. We shall understand Confucius better if we try to see what such a basis might be. We must try to see Confucius's teaching as an imaginative and creative response to social conflict and turmoil, not as merely unimaginative, as persistent blindness to the nature of the crisis of his times.

In the remarks that follow, I do not claim to come up

with new facts—only to tell a familiar story in a new and, I hope, illuminating way.

We must begin by seeing Confucius as a great cultural innovator rather than as a genteel but stubbornly nostalgic apologist of the status quo ante. Just as we have noted elsewhere that he transformed the concept of *li*, so now we must take note that in doing so he transformed the whole concept of human society. He was the creator of a new ideal, not an apologist for an old one.

Let us for a while look at him as the proponent of a new ideal. Let us—initially at least—look at the historical role of his teaching objectively, rather than through his eyes and the surface idiom of his language. He talked in terms of restoring an ancient harmony; but the practical import of his teaching was to lead men to look for new ways of interpreting and refashioning a local tradition in order to bring into being a new, universal order to replace the contemporary disorder.

What Confucius saw were in historical fact the newly *emerging* similarities in social-political practices, the newly *emerging*, widespread sharing of values that had once been restricted to a small region which included Lu. He saw the emerging of widely shared literary forms, musical forms, legal forms and political forms. We, who look at the situation in the light of historical evidence, see that rather than a devolution from some great past civilization, an evolution toward a new and universalistic civilization was taking place. There had been a recent and vast increase in population in the region. There was in progress a leap forward in the techniques of productivity and in the expansion of communications. Numerous previously isolated and culturally differentiated peoples were now in more intimate contact. The interchange and syntheses of ideas, styles, customs and language were taking place on a grand scale.

In short, what Confucius's idiom and imagery portray as the

increasing chaos of a civilization in course of degeneration was, in fact, the inevitable disorder attendant upon the evolution of a new, larger and greater single society out of various older, smaller, culturally separate and more primitive and provincial groups. How natural it was that Confucius should take note of the dominance of his own culture—the culture of Lu and a few surrounding principalities—over the cultures of the much larger and more populous regions which had formerly been more or less isolated and alien societies but which were now merging into a great and growing geopolitical comity. Given the relative physical weakness of tiny Lu, it was a natural tactic for a man of Lu to turn attention not to military conquest but to cultural conquest as the primary basis for order and unity.

We must suppose, in short, that Confucius looked around him and found among the powerful states much conflict but also some signs of acceptance of a culture derivative from the culture of the region of Lu. Next we must suppose that he saw —as an *ideal*—the possibility that all the known peoples might be unified and pacific if all adopted a single, humane set of practices and ideas. Finally, as a man of Lu, he saw that the latter ideal might be achieved by vigorous proselytizing to stimulate and to maximize the tendency, already manifest, to accept the culture of Lu as the framework for the new society.

Confucius's vision was in fact, more than any other, the true vision of the actual future of China. It was a vision of the emergence of a grand and powerful unified culture rooted in a unified polity, the whole deriving its inspiration from a unified literature, language and ceremonial forms of the region of Lu and its environs.

In the circumstances, how could such a *new* ideal be formulated and persuasively taught? Immediately a paradox presents itself. The ideal is of a grand society sharing the same practices and ideas. But what is the source of conventional practices and ways of thought? How are they generated, justified, maintained? Here the Confucian answer is fundamentally twofold. First, there is the emphasis on tradition.

In general terms, there are three ways in which conventional practices may be established: by effective command, by common agreement and by inheritance through accepted tradition. All three are implicitly acknowledged as important by Confucius: the true king leads the way; the people consent and voluntarily follow; what is taught and followed is the *tradition*, the way of the Ancients. Even if the content of tradition is conceived as Heaven's Will (another form of "command") it coincides with the Way of the Ancients, for Heaven's will is not fickle. Recognizing all these, Confucius still gave primacy in his teaching to the Way of the Ancients, to tradition.

Why should he have finally given primary emphasis to tradition? We may note at once some important yet secondary types of reasons. The common people could only follow, never lead—this seemed self-evident because of their obvious lack of knowledge and culture and because of the absence of any tradition suggesting otherwise. Hence consensus of the community could only be a background factor. The rulers, on the other hand, were in historical fact too often arbitrary and power-mad at this period. A good ruler was needed, was indeed conceivable; but to be good the ruler had to have some impersonal standard of goodness. The only candidates for an impersonal standard are tradition or a Divine Command.

Although Confucius did speak of Heaven, its role is not too clear and is unelaborated in the *Analects.* At this point we come to the decisive influence of Confucius's philosophical insights into *man* rather than his insights into politics. He was not impressed with the possibilities of metaphysical speculation and "theology," as we know. But he was deeply concerned with man's life on earth. One of Confucius's chief substantive insights was precisely that man's humanity could be comprehended through the imagery of *li*. He saw that it is well-learned conventional practice that distinguishes man from the beasts and from the inanimate. He saw how miraculous a power, how humane a power was inherent in well-learned conventional practices as distinguished from force, threats and commands. Finally he saw that the dignity peculiar to man and the power associated with this dignity could be characterized in terms of holy rite, of ceremony. For ceremony is a conventionalized practice in which are emphasized intrinsic harmony, beauty and sacredness.

Thus Confucius's new ideal was envisioned explicitly in terms of the imagery of holy rite and ceremony, and these, in turn, are forms of conduct which more than most others are rooted in ancient tradition. Whatever the ultimate psychological or other explanation for it, there is no doubt that the ultimate solemnity of which rite is capable, the deep, archaic response it evokes in man's soul, are never present insofar as any pattern of conduct or gesture is felt to be new, invented, or utilitarian. Although we may with occasional success modify a complex rite, at least the materials or elements of it will be traditional.

Of the various considerations, tacit or explicit, that might well have influenced Confucius, his essentially secular vision of distinctively human nature as rooted in *li* seems to me to have been the decisive specific reason for his coming to apprehend the unity of a great civilization as based primarily on tradition rather than on consensus or command. As has been noted, the ideas of social consensus and of princely or Divine commands could still play a role in Confucius's thought in rationalizing the traditions that define a culture. Nevertheless, their practical role for Confucius would have to be secondary, less elaborated. The central emphasis on *li*—as it has for other thinkers concerned with ceremony—led directly to tradition as the effective emotional-moral authority for *li*, whatever other ideological, philosophical or religious frame might be added.

Thus two great insights fused in Confucius's thought. Confucius, the political man, conceived that the social crisis required cultural unity as an essential ground of a civilized political-social unity. And Confucius, the philosophical anthropologist, affirmed life lived in the image of the authentic ceremonial act as the necessary and sufficient condition of authentic humanity. The implications of these themes taken jointly call for political-social unity to be ceremonial. And this in turn calls for a tradition-oriented culture as essential ground out of which ceremony is nourished.

The paradox faced by Confucius is therefore: How can one present a *new* ideal to people when the ideal is that they should accept a tradition as their own and as a sacred one at that? One has traditions; one does not choose or create them upon need. Clearly there is no way to press an ideal in the form of a tradition except by presenting the new ideal as simply a reaffirmation, an appeal to an ancient, legitimate but neglected tradition.

We must suppose that a thinker of Confucius's time and circumstances could have conceived a nontradition-oriented alternative. Such an alternative was clearly and forcefully expressed by the so-called Legalists as well as by other thinkers whose ideas were already formulated by Confucius's time and must have been known to him. The Legalists, for example, advocated a community governed by regulations enforced by the twin motives of fear and hope of profit. It is essential to see that Confucius was concerned not merely with communal order but with human dignity, with a culture that was founded in a sense of the beautiful, the noble and the sacred as distinctive dimensions of human existence. Cultural unity was to be the consummation of humanity, not an order imposed upon sheep in human form.

We are now prepared to consider the second fundamental element in Confucius's handling of his new ideal of a universalistic community based upon shared conventions. The *content* of his proposal was to found the new community as a tradition. But he also found ready to hand a distinctively suited and powerful *formal* mode of discourse in which to propagate the ideal; indeed he used the most deeply rooted mode of discourse in human culture—the narrative and especially the narrative myth or anecdote of an ancient past.

Societies have varied in their characteristic way of formulating abstract and especially spiritual issues, but one approach is shared by all and is historically the earliest: the use of narrative. We have various names for such narratives—"history," "myth," "folktale." In these narrative forms, the moral, legal, spiritual or psychological aspects of birth, for example, are presented not by means of abstract concepts but in terms of a myth of birth—i.e., a narrative portraying events and personages. The narrative may be spoken, acted out or written. Death, mating, work, personal relationships, the place of man in the world—these issues are in every society approached in terms of narrative. In a few cultures, such as European, Indian and Chinese civilizations, we also find abstract, theoretical doctrine or analysis applied to these issues.

To cope with the *meaning* of life rather than its physical realities, man has always begun by apprehending that meaning not in the form of an abstract conception about this life but in the form of a narrative of events in some way parallel to it. This parallel world may be told of as concurrent with the present but going on in a different realm (Heaven, Mount Olympus). Or it may be presented as a narrative of events here near our home on earth but prior to our times; or it may be a narrative of events presented as both in an earlier time and in some other realm. The shift of the narrative to another time or place, and the idealized (or extreme) character of the beings and their powers and deeds, have sufficed to free the narrative of inconsistency with the narrative drawn from recent and genuine memory of human beings and events. The interaction of the "other" realm and our own represents the way in which the meaning of our life both transcends and also is embodied in the day-to-day events of this life.

Since the memory narrative gives history as memory, and the other gives history as meaning, both can be in their way valid—what they tell is so. Memory narrative leads into the present, and so does the meaning narrative. Moreover meaning and memory cannot be kept entirely distinct; each requires the other and blends into it. Thus the distinction which we often make between history as true and myth as false is one to which many groups are blind. The distinction is in the first instance oversharp, easily misleading. Insofar as the "myth" narrative is felt as distinctive from the memory narrative, this is often because the former is *more* significant, more enduringly valid. For the myth narrative explains, justifies, illuminates our life on earth. As that that gives meaning, that *is* the meaning, it is more important in its way than life as naïvely apprehended by one unacquainted with the relevant myth. The "other" realm is always the source of significance as well as the realm of being of significance.

Such meaning narratives are typically doubly historical. Being narrative in form, they present us with the meaning of life displayed as a series of meaningfully connected events in time —a piece of history, in short. In addition, as we have noted, their "otherness" or "transcendence" is readily represented in the narrative mode by locating the total story either in a distant past, or in a distant place, or in both. For the man of modern European civilization who worships what I have called memory narrative as against meaning narrative, the meaning is tacitly blended into the memory—that is, what we call history is, so to speak, our myth. And, as we learn increasingly, what are on the surface meaning narratives, myths, tend to be rooted in actual past events which had in some way impinged upon the society in which the myth plays its role.

When the narrative that gives significance is located in a distant past, it is usually a past that the narrative itself eventually links up with the historical past, the remembered historical past. Elaborate narrative and genealogy usually link the truly historical past with that "other" ("ancient") past; though not infrequently we find that the beings of the other realm continue their own history parallel to the emerging human history, though normally invisible during waking human life.

In spite of the invention of abstract theory and conceptual analysis, the inclination to this use of narrative has by no means disappeared in Western civilization. True enough, we have often been slaves to theoretical ideologies, doctrines and slogans ("free speech," "the rights of man"). Yet we remain dedicated not only to the study of what we call history (which puts remembered past into meaningful order), but also to religious narrative, political myth-making, commercial "personalizing" and "testimonials," and to drama, art and literature as modes of thought and sensibility for the exploration of life's meaning.

Confucius, on independent grounds, perceived humanity through the imagery of ceremony and hence of tradition. It was peculiarly appropriate for him to turn to the narrative mode of formulation in its most common form—the narrative of an ancient past. Thus the content of his teaching was perfectly congenial to the oldest and probably the most evocative of all forms of thinking about life's meaning. Although the narrative mode used in this way is an "archaic" form of thought, it is not any more an archaism in Confucius than it is in a contemporary novel or drama. Confucius used the narrative of a mythic past in the service of a new ideal grounded in radically new insights into man's essential nature and powers.

Thus, in Confucius's thought, the formal mode (narrative of a meaning-generating "past") fused with the content of his teaching (the crucial role of tradition); he could talk in a way that was perfectly suited to arouse that deep reverence and loyalty to tradition that was the content of his ideal.

To see Confucius's teaching in this light is to rescue it from the status of a historical curiosity for Western man and to keep it as a teaching with relevance to all men. We began by considering the problem of culture conflict for one who teaches a "return" to the Ancient Way. But now we see that the teaching need not require having a tradition that is both authentically historical, internally coherent and totally adequate. Instead, the burden of the teaching can be what in effect it was as Confucius taught it: to seek inspiration in one's own traditions in such a way as to reveal a humanizing and harmonizing interpretation for the conflictful present. "He who by reanimating the Old can gain knowledge of the New is indeed fit to be called a teacher."(2:11)

The aim of "reanimating the Old" may seem to be a euphemism for irresponsible or self-serving tinkering with actual traditions, a species of hypocrisy and rationalization. Confucius certainly denied this. He claimed, "I have been faithful to and loved the Ancients." (7:1) That is, the interpretation of tradition had to be rooted in a genuine love and respect for one's past. Confucius, Jesus, Gautama Buddha are examples of men who genuinely and profoundly and self-consciously reanimated their traditions; but the many Confucians, Christians, and Buddhists who merely pick and choose among the bits of tradition for whatever saying or practice suits their present purposes represent the natural (but not inevitable) misuse of this approach. And those who hold rigidly and uncritically to traditional forms and ceremonies, no matter how inadequate these may be to the present, are likewise to be contrasted with these three profound reanimators of their traditions.

The constant reanimation of the Old as a way of knowing what is new is not a parochial ideal. It has relevance for all men always. For it is an expression of a valid insight into what humanity is. Man has the peculiar power and dignity that he has by virtue of being able to act in intelligently conventional ways rather than out of instinct or conditioning alone. (This is no more than very many of our most influential philosophic analysts tell us today.) The forms of life, even when viewed in their aspect as intelligent convention, cannot be invented and accepted en bloc; they rest primarily on the inheritance by each age of a vast body of conventional language and practices from the preceding age. Only as we grow up genuinely shaped, through and through, by traditional ways can we be human; only as we reanimate this tradition where new circumstances render it otiose can we preserve integrity and direction in our life. Shared tradition brings men together, enables them to be men. Every abandonment of tradition is a separation of men. Every authentic reanimation of tradition is a reuniting of men.

The vision of an emerging unity among men was thus not merely a political vision—though even as such this Confucian vision was one of the most grandiose—and successful—of any political vision in recorded history. But it was a philosophical vision, even a religious one. It revealed humanity, sacred and marvelous, as residing in community, community as rooted in the inherited forms of life.

Our contemporary world is only too understandably and justifiably oriented toward novelty, frenetic change and crisis. In such a world Confucius's fundamental vision of man may yet not be an anachronism. It may be that, for just such a world, Confucius's perspective is more relevant, more timely, more urgent than it ever was in the later and all-too tradition-bound China which we see as its natural habitat. It is because it is so alien to our times that we need to penetrate the truth of Confucius's vision; it is because it is so alien to the times that we tend to be impatient with it and blind to its truth.

5

A Confucian Metaphor
—the Holy Vessel

What is it that distinguishes man from the beasts and the inanimate? In what do man's peculiar dignity and power reside? Confucius offers an amazingly apt and generative image: Rite *(li)*. But Rite and Ceremony would seem, off hand, to deemphasize the individual, whereas the tendency in much modern criticism is to stress the "discovery of the individual"[1] by Confucius. It is true that Hughes, who uses this particular phrase, adds a qualifying clause "man's ability to look at himself in relation to his fellows and in that light to integrate himself."

Wing-tsit Chan summarizes in a similar formula "the entire Confucian philosophy: . . . the realization of the self and the creation of a social order."[2] Although Hughes and Chan bring out the two poles "individual"–"society," Liu Wu-chi emphasizes even more the "individual" pole: "No matter from which angle we view it, the individual man is, after all, the hub of the universe. . . . Master K'ung discovered by a happy stroke of genius the ethical individual. . . . Individual man was now exalted to his new position as a social entity. . . . Thus for the

---

1. Hughes, *Individual in East and West*, p. 94.
2. Wing-tsit Chan, "The Story of Chinese Philosophy," *Philosophy—East and West*, ed., C.A. Moore (Princeton: Princeton University Press, 1944), p. 27.

first time in the history of man, the dignity of the individual was asserted. . . . The flowering of the individual is to be one's ultimate aim."[3] Creel, although he too elaborates on the social orientation of Confucius, nevertheless emphasizes in various contexts the "primacy and worth of the individual" in Confucius's thought.[4] And Lin Yutang, while stressing the social, says " . . . the kingdom of God is truly within man himself."[5]

In short, in these passages from a representative sample of modern writers we see a broadly recurring pattern of interpretation. In citing such brief phrases, one wrenches the remarks from contexts in which there is essential qualification and amplification. My aim in quoting, however, is not to provide a rounded report of the commentaries, but rather to note that when a brief and summary formula is finally required, the formula often tends to be formulated in terms of "society" and the "individual," with relative emphasis on the "individual" as primary. Self-realization, self-integrity, "self-flowering," the "ultimate worth of the individual"—these are supposed to reflect the characteristic discovery of Confucius. It is the thesis of the present remarks that we would do better to think of Confucius as concerned with the nature of "humanity" rather than with

3. Liu Wu-chi, *Confucius*, pp. 155–56
4. Creel, *Confucius and the Chinese Way*, pp. 136, 138. My own interpretation follows Creel (and in some ways Kaizuka) more than most in the way they stress the inseparability of man from society and the role of *li*. Without wishing to minimize this similarity or to enter into detailed comparative commentary, I might simply say that I have attempted to draw the philosophical and psychological implications of this view more stringently and more fully. I think that doing this puts Confucius's position in a new light. For one thing it helps to bring out the close logical connection between this view of man and the magical-reverential dimension of Confucius's thought—a dimension that I believe is seriously understated by Creel and "rationalized" (in spite of his evident *feeling* for it). See also: H.G. Creel, *Chinese Thought from Confucius to Mao Tse-Tung* (New York: New American Library, 1960), pp. 33–34.
5. Lin Yutang, *Wisdom of Confucius*, p. 17.

the polar terms "individual" and "society." The formulation in terms of individual and society reflects Western preoccupations and categories—and perhaps Taoist, Buddhist and neo-Confucian concerns.

Rather than arguing this point in the abstract, we cannot do better than to learn from Confucius himself, and more particularly from reflection on one of the illuminating images he presents to us.

Tzu-Kung asked: "What would you say about me as a person?"
The Master said: "You are a utensil."
"What sort of utensil?"
"A sacrificial vase of jade." (5:3)

This passage is usually read in the light of another passage in the *Analects* (2:11): "A noble man is not a utensil."

The general opinion among commentators, in the light of 2:11, seems to have been that Confucius is first putting Tzu-Kung in his place, and then, in his next response, softening the blow. These interpreters (whom I believe to be mistaken) might be supposed to read the cryptic passage along the lines of the following paraphrase.

"Master," we may suppose Tzu-Kung to be saying, "tell me where I stand with regard to the ideal." The Master replies, "You are still only a utensil, useful only for specific purposes. You are not the morally self-realized man, the man with broad (moral) capacities who is capable of governing or using the special (technical) capacities of others." Tzu-Kung, his eagerness and optimism shaken, does not give up. "But, Master, how do you mean that? Don't you have some qualifying or softening word with which you can give me more hope?" And the Master replies, in a paternalistic, encouraging tone: "Tzu-Kung, don't feel too bad about it. Even if you are still a man to be used and not yet one who is perfected and capable of using others, at least you are a very fine utensil of your kind. Indeed you are among the most handsome and valuable."

In my own opinion, as I have indicated, a reading along such lines is quite wrong. The only element of it that is acceptable is that Confucius does initially intend to dash cold water on Tzu-Kung's too-ready optimism. Confucius wants to bring him up short, to shake him, disturb him, puzzle him; Tzu-Kung must be made to feel the necessity to *think* his way through to a new insight. Confucius puts his answer in a manner best calculated to accomplish this end with a man of Tzu-Kung's character. It seems that this disciple was the most facilely successful and worldly of Confucius's disciples. With his learning and his worldly success, he might well feel pride in his personal achievement, might well be surprised and shaken at Confucius's initial response. For Tzu-Kung is well aware of the metaphor of the utensil and of the saying that a noble man is *not* a utensil. Confucius's initial response, like others he makes, is the first element, then, in a pedagogically effective paradox.[6]

However, the second statement by Confucius—"You are a sacrificial vessel of jade"—is not a mere sentimental softening of the blow. It both completes and resolves the paradox. It contains in a highly condensed image the central teaching which Confucius wishes to get across to the glib and self-satisfied Tzu-Kung. What is this central teaching?

Consider the sacrificial vessel: in the original text Confucius merely names a certain type of jade sacrificial vessel used for holding grain in connection with ceremonies for a bounteous

6. For examples of Confucius's readiness to let an ironic comment stand without softening if irony is his intent and for his use of challenging, puzzling or paradoxical statements, see, for example, 3:8; 5:3; 6:1; 6:10; 6:22; 6:23; 7:10; 7:29; 10:26; 11:17; 11:21.

harvest. Such a vessel is holy, sacred. Its outer appearance—
the bronze, the carving, the jade—is elegant. Its content, the
rich grain, expresses abundance.

Yet the vessel's sacredness does not reside in the pre-
ciousness of its bronze, in the beauty of its ornamentation,
in the rarity of its jade or in the edibility of the grain.
Whence does its sacredness come? It is sacred not because
it is useful or handsome but because it is a constitutive element in the ceremony. It is sacred by virtue of its participation in rite, in holy ceremony. In isolation from its role
in the ceremony, the vessel is merely an expensive pot
filled with grain.

It is therefore a paradox as utensil, for unlike utensils in
general, this has no (utilitarian) use external to ceremony
itself but only a ritual function. (Indeed some ceremonial
pots had holes in them in order to emphasize their ritual
rather than utilitarian value.)

By analogy, Confucius may be taken to imply that the individual human being, too, has ultimate dignity, sacred dignity by virtue of his role in rite, in ceremony, in *li*. We
must recall that Confucius expanded the sense of the word
li, originally referring to religious ceremonial, in such a
way as to envision society itself on the model of *li*. If the
teaching about *li* is thus generalized, it is reasonable to follow through and generalize the analogy between Tzu-Kung
and the ceremonial vessel. We will then see how this image
deepens our understanding of Confucius's teaching about
man and human relations.

Social etiquette in general, the father-son relation, the
brother-brother relation, the prince-subject relation, the
friend-friend relation and the husband-wife relation—persons and their relationships are to be seen as ultimately
sanctified by virtue of their place in *li*. Society, at least in-

sofar as regulated by human convention and moral obligations, becomes in the Confucian vision one great ceremonial
performance, a ceremony with all the holy beauty of an elaborate religious ritual carried out with that combination of
solemnity and lightness of heart that graces the inspired ritual
performance. It is not individual existence *per se*, nor is it the
existence of a group *per se* that is the condition sufficient to
create and sustain the ultimate dignity of man. It is the ceremonial aspect of life that bestows sacredness upon persons,
acts, and objects which have a role in the performance of
ceremony.

Confucius does not see the individual as an ultimate atom
nor society on the analogy of animal or mechanism, nor does
he see society as a proving ground for immortal souls or a
contractual or utilitarian arrangement designed to maximize
individual pleasure. He does not talk in the *Analects* of society
and the individual. He talks of what it is to be man, and he sees
that man is a special being with a unique dignity and power
deriving from and embedded in *li*.

Is it enough merely to be born, to eat, breathe, drink, ex-
crete, enjoy sensual gratification and avoid physical pain and
discomfort? Animals do this. To become civilized is to establish relationships that are not merely physical, biological or
instinctive; it is to establish *human* relationships, relationships
of an essentially symbolic kind, defined by tradition and convention and rooted in respect and obligation.

"Merely to feed one's parents well" . . . "even dogs and
horses are fed." (2:7) To be devoted to one's parents is far more
than to keep the parents alive physically. To serve and eat in
the proper way, with the proper respect and appreciation, in
the proper setting—this is to transform the act of mere nour-
ishment into the human ceremony of dining. To obey the
whip is to be not much more than a domestic animal; but to

be loyal and faithful to those who rightly govern, to serve them and thus to serve *in* the human community, to do this out of one's own heart and nature—this is to be a true citizen of one's community.

Man's dignity, as does the dignity of things, lies in the ceremony rather than in individual biological existence, and this is evident in the fact that we understand a man who sacrifices his biological existence, his "life" in the biological but not the spiritual sense, if the "rite" demands it. Confucius makes the point succinctly when he responds to his disciple's concern over killing a sheep as an element in a sacrificial rite: "You love the sheep, but I love the ceremony," says Confucius. (3:17)

"Virtue does not exist in isolation; there must be neighbors," says Confucius.(4:25) Man is transformed by participation with others in ceremony which is communal. Until he is so transformed he is not truly man but only potentially so— the new-born infant the wolf-boy of the forests or the "barbarian." Ceremony is justified when we see how it transforms the barbarian into what we know as man at his best. And, from the opposite direction, man at his best is justified when we see that his best is a life of holy ceremony rather than of appetite and mere animal existence. Whichever standpoint we take, we get a perspective on man and society which illuminates and deepens our vision of man's distinctive nature and dignity. When we see man as participant in communal rite rather than as individualistic ego, he takes on to our eyes a new and holy beauty just as does the sacrificial vessel.

Thus, in the *Analects*, man as individual is not sacred. However, he is not therefore to be thought of as a mere utensil to serve "society." For society is no more an independent entity than is ceremony independent of the participants, the holy vessels, the altar, the incantations. Society is men treating each other as men (*jen*), or to be more specific, according to the obligations and privileges of *li*, out of the love (*ai*) and loyalty

(chung) and respect *(shu)* called for by their human relationships to each other. The shapes of human relationships are not
imposed on man, not physically inevitable, not an instinct or
reflex. They are rites learned and voluntarily participated in.
The rite is self-justifying. The beings, the gestures, the words
are not subordinate to rite, nor is rite subordinate to them. To
"be self-disciplined and ever turning to *li*" (12:1) is to be no
longer at the mercy of animal needs and demoralizing passion,
it is to achieve that freedom in which the human spirit flowers;
it is not, as Waley's translation may lead one to think, a matter
of "submission" but of the triumph of the human spirit.

Confucius's theme, then, is not the "discovery of the individual" or of his ultimate importance. The *mere* individual is
a bauble, malleable and breakable, a utensil transformed into
the resplendent and holy as it serves in the ceremony of life.
But then this does not deny *ultimate* dignity to men and to each
man; he is not a meaningless ant serving the greater whole. His
participation in divinity is as real and clearly visible as is that
of the sacrificial vessel, for it *is* holy. And unlike the way he
appears in the Christian view, man is not holy by virtue of his
absolute possession, within himself and independently of
other men, of a "piece" of the divine, the immortal soul. Nor
is the "flowering" of the individual the central theme; instead
it is the flowering of humanity in the ceremonial acts of men.

Although the individual must cultivate himself, just as the
temple vessel must be carved and chiseled and polished, this
self-cultivation is no more *central* to man's dignity, in Confucius's views, than the preparation of the vessel is central.
Preparation and training are essential, but it is the ceremony
that is central, and *all* the elements and relationships and
actions in it are sacred though each has its special characteris-
tics.

Nor should we suppose that Nature is cast out unless shaped
into artifact for ritual use. The raiment of holiness is cast upon

Nature as well as man, upon the river and the air as well as upon youth and song, when these are seen through the image of a ceremonial Rain Dance. (11:25)

The noble man is the man who most perfectly having given up self, ego, obstinacy and personal pride (9:4) follows not profit but the Way. Such a man has come to fruition as a person; he is the consummate Man. He is a Holy Vessel.

Note on Textual Matters

For the purposes of this book, I refer to the views of Confucius and mean thereby the teachings ascribed to him in the classic collection of his sayings, the *Analects*. More specifically, I have turned to those portions of the *Analects* that are thought likely to be earlier and closer to the authentic sayings of Confucius himself. Of course it has been doubted whether any of the sayings in the *Analects* were actually Confucius's, and there seems good reason to suppose that they are at least worked-over versions of his actual words. Nevertheless, the consensus seems to be that much of the *Analects* constitutes the largest single body of quotations or near-quotations from the historical Confucius. In any case, it is the doctrine to be found in this work that is central to my purpose, not the precise historical origin of it.

As to the identification of this "earliest core" itself, there are differences of opinion. So far as I know, there is a consensus among experts that Chapters 3 through 8 are to be included (certain particular passages excepted). With individual differences of opinion, there is broadly a consensus that if we go beyond this central core and take larger and larger segments of the work (2–9; 1–9; 1–15; 1–20), we get increasingly greater amounts of materials that are later in style and at times, but not always, foreign in content to Confucius's sayings and ideas. I have consulted especially James Legge, "*Confucian Analects*" in *The Chinese Classics*; Arthur Waley, *The Analects of Confucius*; H. G. Creel, *Confucius and the Chinese Way* and his *Literary Chinese by the Inductive Method II*; Daniel Leslie, *Confucius* and his article in *T'oung Pao*, "Notes on the Analects"; and S. Kaizuka, *Confucius*.

Quotations from the *Analects* are cited by Chapter and paragraph according to the traditional text. There are a number of English translations that follow this order, the two most useful being Legge's and Waley's (cited above). Legge's is the "classic" English source. Waley's is a modern one, outstanding both in style and scholarship. The quotations as given in this paper are basically Legge's and Waley's with occasional contributions by myself. Where I have modified or retranslated, my aim has been to reduce the interpretive element, and to reproduce or approximate the original imagery of the Chinese text in a way that would be intelligible in English.

Bibliography

(Works occasionally consulted or cited are identified in full in the footnotes.)

BODDE, D. "A Perplexing Passage in the Confucian *Analects.*" *Jo. Amer. Oriental Society,* 1933, 53: 347–351.

CHAN, WING-TSIT. *A Source Book in Chinese Philosophy.* Princeton: Princeton University Press, 1963.

COUVREUR, F. S. *Dictionnaire Classique de la Langue Chinoise.* Reprint. Taiwan: Book World Company, 1963.

COUVREUR, F. S. *Entretiens de Confucius et de ses Disciples. Les Quatre Livres.* Paris: Cathasia, n.d.

CREEL, H. G. *Confucius and the Chinese Way.* New York: Harper & Row, Torchbook No. 63, 1960.

CREEL, H. G. "Was Confucius Agnostic?" *T'oung Pao,* 1932, 29:55–99.

CREEL, LORRAINE. *The Concept of Social Order in Early Confucianism.* University of California Library, 1946. (Photographic Reproductions)

DUBS, H. H. " 'Nature' in the Teaching of Confucius." *Jo. Amer. Oriental Society,* 1930, 50:233–237.

FUNG YU-LAN. *A History of Chinese Philosophy.* translated by D. Bodde. Vol. I, Princeton: Princeton University Press, 1952.

GILES, HERBERT A. *A Chinese-English Dictionary.* London: Kelly & Walsh, 1912.

GILES, L. *The Sayings of Confucius.* New York: Grove Press, 1961.

HUGHES, E. R. *Chinese Philosophy in Classical Times.* New York: E. P. Dutton, 1942.

———, ed. *The Individual in East & West.* London: Oxford University Press, 1937.

KAIZUKA, S. *Confucius.* translated by G. Bournes. London: George Allen & Unwin, 1956.

KARLGREN, B. *Analytic Dictionary of Chinese & Sino-Japanese.* Paris: Librairie Orientaliste Paul Geuthner, 1923.

LAUFER, B. "Lun Yu IX, i." *Jo. Amer. Oriental Society*, 1934, 54:83.

LEGGE, JAMES. *Confucian Analects. The Chinese Classics.* Reprint. Hong Kong: Hong Kong University Press, 1960.

LESLIE, DANIEL. *Confucius.* Paris: Editions Seghers, 1962.

———. "Notes on the *Analects.*" *T'oung Pao*, 1961, 49:54–63.

LIN YUTANG. *The Wisdom of Confucius.* New York: Random House, Modern Library, 1938.

LIU WU-CHI. *Confucius, His Life & Times.* New York: Philosophical Library, 1955.

MATHEWS, R. H. *Chinese-English Dictionary.* rev. ed. (American). Cambridge, Mass: Harvard University Press, 1960.

POUND, EZRA. "The *Analects* of Confucius." *Hudson Review*, Vol. 3, Spring & Summer, 1950.

SOOTHILL, W. E. *The Analects.* London: Oxford University Press, 1958.

WALEY, ARTHUR. *The Analects of Confucius.* New York: Random House, Modern Library, No. P-66, 1938.

WARE, JAMES R. *The Sayings of Confucius.* New York: New American Library, Mentor Classic, 1955.

74 75   12 11 10 9 8 7 6 5 4 3 2